Life
and other problems

Life
and other problems

Clarice Hoffer Thompson

graphics and layout by Jack Thompson

ISBN 13 978-1477510476
      10 1477510478

CONTENTS

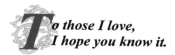 *o those I love,
I hope you know it.*

*To those who love,
who struggle,
who are unsure,
and those who are absolutely sure,
this collection is about you.*

Thanks to dear Jack, for being Jack

A Midwest Woman

*I*n 2007 The Williamston Theatre was planning a play to be called "Maidens, Mothers and Crones," based on the voices of women of the Midwest. In order to develop this idea, they sent questionnaires to women in various parts of the Midwest asking them to share stories of their lives and dreams. When I began to work on my answers I knew I was well versed

in maidens and mothers. Crones? Not yet, I hoped. Two out of three might do the job.

Months later I saw the play. I enjoyed it, but couldn't tell whether any of my submissions had actually made it to the performance. Now, four years later, I find them on my computer. Here's what they asked, along with my responses written in 2007:

1. Tell us about your hair.

My hair is 75 years old. No, that isn't accurate. It is really about 73. For the first two years I didn't have any hair. My mother bought a cloth-covered elastic band sporting a large plaid bow. This presumably prevented strangers from saying, "Cute little fella!"

One memorable day when I was about 16 years old, I had good hair. I mean *really* good – shiny, gently curling. I looked just like the Breck girl in my *Seventeen* magazine ads.

It had never happened before, and it has never happened again. Ever.

Over the years I have spent about 50 thousand hours and 20 thousand dollars on my hair. And the ungrateful stuff still refuses to co-operate.

You know what's really sad? On that day that I had perfect hair, it only lasted for about an hour. Then the wind kicked up, and that was the end of that.

2a. What will your legacy be?

Legacy. What a word! To think of the trail of mistakes and misadventures that I might be leaving behind is really quite scary.

A priest told my husband that the only sins were sins of intention. That's a comforting thought. I don't think I ever intentionally hurt anyone. Well, there was that one time in first grade . . . .

2b. What would you LIKE your legacy to be?

I'd like to be remembered as someone who knew how to celebrate being alive. Once my daughter, in college at the time, sent me a beautiful card. On the front she wrote, "Mom, Thanks for not sweating the small stuff." And inside she said, "Thanks for not sweating the big stuff, either."

That's enough legacy for me.

3. How do you know you have value?

I think I got that from my parents. When I was young I dried the glasses and silverware while my mother washed all the dishes. We let the crockery and pots dry by themselves. Often Mom and I sang duets, "There's a Long, Long Trail (a-winding)," or, "Tell Me Why the Stars Do Shine," and more. It was beautiful. Maybe not. Didn't matter.

Mom and I worked on the laundry, pegging out clothes on warm summer days. Dad "needed" me to help with tasks such as minor repairs around the house and yard. My job was to select and pass to him the proper tools. Dad let me know that I was needed, which I probably wasn't.

4. Describe the average schedule of your day.

I am retired and do as I please when I please. I volunteer, read trash, write trash (that I hope isn't), and concentrate on savoring every bit of the time I have left. The days fly by, but never without my noticing what's good about them. And there's a lot of good. Finding it helps balance all the bad that tirelessly tries to claim our attention.

5. When I was a little girl, I wanted to . . .

Grow up, get married and have babies. Hey, it was the 1940s. The choices of career for girls ("In case you don't get married") were teacher or nurse. That would serve as fulfillment.

I did it, too. I got married, had babies and became a teacher. It wasn't bad at all. I doubt that I was nuclear scientist material, anyway. It's a different world now, for girls. And I think that is a very good thing.

6. If I had an extra hour, I would . . .

Treasure it. I do have extra hours these days, as an old person, and I do treasure them, all of them. If things seem to be getting slow, I hoist myself up and do something productive. Nothing like it for keeping the blahs at bay. The term "productive" can mean anything from reading something beautiful to tossing out the wilted lettuce in the fridge. The end result is surprisingly similar for both activities.

7. I feel beautiful when . . .

I smile at strangers and they smile back. I pick someone at random, in a store or on the street and play a game – noticing how they look before, during and after their smiles. I have never met anyone who did not look beautiful smiling.

8. I feel ugly when . . .

I can't get myself past being angry about something. Sometimes the anger is from years ago. Nothing very pretty about that. But it's my choice, and ugly people get to choose to remain ugly. You just don't want to look in the mirror at times like that.

Our mothers knew what they were talking about when they said, "Watch out, your face might freeze!"

tar Light

In the dark kitchen
through the window
the morning star glistens,
alone in black space.
Something inside me,
near my heart,
soars up to meet it, rests there for a moment
and returns.

I am insignificant,
tiny in a universe where even that star is miniscule.

I turn from the window,
reassured, stronger.
My tiny world
almost in order.

Life in 4/4 Time

December 2004

*E*ach season has its rhythm and, although we are mostly unaware of it, we slow dance to the beat along with the other flora and fauna that share our planet.

Around Thanksgiving I begin to act as instinctively as the southbound songbird. I'm impelled toward behaviors unthinkable in the heat and storms of August: Where did I store the down comforter? Let's put up the storm door. Which boxes have the outdoor lights and Christmas wreaths and bows?

On the day before Thanksgiving this year everyone was well warned of approaching snow. A sense of urgency prompted my husband and me to search the house for the makings of our modest outdoor display – a lighted reindeer on the back deck, garlands and lights edging the front door and wrapping the porch railings. Through splatting half-frozen drops we made a run to Home Depot to buy an outdoor timer and new heavy duty extension cords. At bedtime when we walked outside to check our work, we delighted in the five or six inches of new snow that decorated even the tiniest twigs with thick icing. Our lights were modest but nice, we agreed. We've said this for each of the eleven years I have lived back in Michigan; back in my childhood home town; back with the seasons.

For more than 40 years in California, I sorely missed seasons. My inborn rhythms caused pangs of longing for I-didn't-know-what on nights when I'd wake in Los Angeles hearing the electric fan drone in the window. Was it December? July? No way to tell. I used to hope that we'd at least have clouds on Christmas day. In subdued light the tree has less competition for its magic twinkling. But invariably we woke to fog followed by brilliant sunshine.

This year, as always, I know my baking gene will kick in soon. I'll stock up on pecans, eggs, food coloring – yeast, even. Some of those things will still be unopened next July, but having them available is suddenly very important. On ambitious years, platefuls of cookies go to the neighbors. Other years they get things that aren't homemade – perhaps chocolate Santas or loaves of fancy bakery bread.

This is the time to of year to appreciate and thank good friends and neighbors.

Why not all year? The rhythm doesn't seem to demand it with the same intensity as it does at holiday time.

Eventually spring arrives and I think, "This is the best season of all." There are fragile baby leaves, baby geese, baby everythings. We feel warmth, rebirth, the joy of opening every window and door to drive out winter air. In comatose gardens, bulbs begin to poke through the soil. Before we know it, masses of blooms are everywhere. There's a certain joy in washing blankets, putting away sweaters and snow shovels; in leaving a restaurant without having to flail around putting on a coat, hoping a sleeve doesn't fly into someone's entrée. Spring is sun on your face, raking up winter debris for the city's free pickup day.

But almost immediately, it seems, comes summer.

In summer it is hard to visualize snow, comforters, warm robes. In the closet my irrelevant-looking wooly slippers gather dust as I put on flip-flops. Christmas seems as remote as life in ancient Egypt.

Summer is bugs on the windshield, lawn sprinklers, fireflies, lightning and thunder. Summer is sitting outside chatting while the evening darkens and cools and drowsy birds chirp themselves to sleep.

Summer is breeze-blown curtains, raucous morning birds claiming their territories; it is driving with the windows down, road maps, being thrown out of the woods by mosquitoes who think they belong there and have a right to eat.

Soon cool weather banishes the mosquitoes, and the trees lose their chlorophyl in the most beautiful ways imaginable. "This is the best season of all," I think, walking in a maple's burnished brilliance. The glow enters the body, imparts magic, quickens the senses. The sky is never bluer than in the fall, the nights never more crisp, the smell of wood smoke never as sweet. Piles of crisp fallen leaves are so enticing that I'm sure ninety-year-olds must scuff through them. Fall is the time to search out sandhill cranes feeding in dry cornfields, to put away garden hoses and cover prized plants before the approaching frost. There's no more mowing, no more air conditioning. Outside we hear geese overhead calling instructions to each other. Songbirds are packing their things, taking the kids and heading south.

Ah, the South. We had a relative who retired to Florida. "Another day in Paradise," he loved to say, congratulating himself for being clever enough to live in almost unrelenting heat. Florida was his paradise.

Fine.

But my paradise is snow clinging to a twig that yesterday sported a brilliant red leaf, that last spring unfurled a baby leaf, that in summer was a billionth part of the shade we enjoyed. Paradise is watching it all happen, feeling it happen. It is the rhythm of the seasons.

Care to dance?

The War Effort

*O*ne winter morning in 1942 we watched the sun rise in the east as our Bailey School classroom brightened sufficiently for us to turn off the lights, saving energy. East Lansing, Michigan was on war time. In the fall all clocks had been set back two hours instead of the usual one. We fifth-graders couldn't fully grasp the concept that getting up before dawn and walking to school in the dark would save energy, but

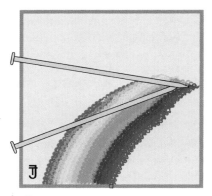

we were willing. Anything for the war effort.

Our country had entered World War II and everyone was saving tin cans, kitchen fat, rags and yarn. The connection between fat and explosives wasn't clear to us children, but we saved it and the other things, along with coins to buy defense stamps.

Everyone knew the phrase, "Is this trip really necessary?" Our class members understood gasoline rationing very well, partly because we walked or bicycled whenever possible. Shoes were rationed, as were butter, coffee and sugar. Meat was a treat, macaroni a staple.

On this particular morning our teacher, Miss Holshuh, beamed at us as she made a special announcement. We were going to learn to knit!

The boys in our class weren't too sure about this knitting business, but Miss Holshuh couched it in terms that bore no argument.

We would knit squares that would be joined to make a blanket. The blanket would be sent to a military hospital to keep a wounded soldier warm. The squares, she told us, would be about 8 inches and the end product would neatly fit a hospital bed. We were to bring left-over yarn from our homes to be distributed and shared.

Knitting time probably was unrecognizable to anyone who actually knew how to knit. We drove our poor teacher almost to distraction, calling upon her to unravel monumental snarls, pick up dropped stitches and show us again and again how to cast on and, eventually, off.

She persevered, however, and finally everyone had made a square – or a trapezoid, triangle, rectangle, rhomboid, amoeba, hourglass, a shape of some sort. Miss Holshuh wasn't quibbling. She had lowered her expectations considerably between the planning and construction phases.

When she could take it no longer, she regarded our heap of mauve, puce, purple, red, navy, rainbow, black, Kelly green, ocher and other-colored freeform wool objects. She managed a brave smile. "Now, whose mother will sew our blanket together?" she asked, implying that this was the highest of all possible honors. She was a master teacher, no doubt about that.

"Mine will!" I cried happily. Me, the kid who at the drop of a hat would volunteer dozens of cookies, buckets of lilacs, transportation—whatever was needed. It never occurred to me not to volunteer my mother, and she never disappointed.

Mother and I laid the 'squares' out on the living room floor. She looked increasingly grim as I pulled each contribution out of the sack I had toted home. I'm sure she was calculating the possibility of whipping up a quick afghan and passing it off as ours, but she knew that wouldn't work. We would be looking for our own contributions. Our little hearts would break if they weren't included.

She worked for days, crocheting between huge gaps, desperately trying to reconcile knitting so tight that it would barely peel off the needle with knitting so loose you could drive a tent peg between stitches. The nightmarish color combinations had, finally, to be ignored as she managed to cram every one of our efforts into some semblance of a blanket. The task consumed several weeks, if I remember correctly.

When I took the finished product to school, our class was ecstatic. Love is blind, and we loved what we had created.

Looking back, I wonder if Miss Holshuh actually had the nerve to mail our blanket to an army hospital. If she did, and if it was given to a wounded soldier, his wounds had better have been bodily ones. One look surely would have pushed a shell-shocked GI into serious relapse.

I can imagine the hospital staff unwrapping our package and collapsing into hysterical laughter. I hope they would have been able to say, "Well, bless their hearts. They meant well." My mother would have deserved at least that much.

A Recent Memory of
a Long-Gone Era

A few years ago on a lovely fall day, my husband, Jack, and I were driving along Chandler Road. It was the afternoon of November 21, 1998.

"Look!" I said, "They're pulling banners from behind those trees."

A football game was about to begin at the Michigan State University stadium. For years

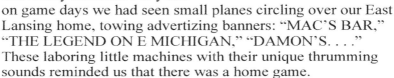

on game days we had seen small planes circling over our East Lansing home, towing advertizing banners: "MAC'S BAR," "THE LEGEND ON E MICHIGAN," "DAMON'S. . . ." These laboring little machines with their unique thrumming sounds reminded us that there was a home game.

We turned west on Clark Road and found a dirt track beside a wide cleared swath that climbed a gentle hill. Several cars were parked at random and a crew of men and women were unrolling banners, setting them out in rows on the stubble.

"Is it OK if we watch?" we asked.

"Nope," said a man who appeared to be the field marshal. "But we can put you to work!"

"Really?" I was thrilled.

"Well, we might need you," he said. "Sometimes they twist going up and the plane has to circle around and drop them in that corn field." He pointed behind a row of trees to a field of dry cornstalks. "Then somebody has to go fetch them."

We were ready!

Two tall skinny poles were mounted on the crest of the hill, a goal-post width apart. Across the top a loop of cable stretched between them. The cable was attached to a banner. A tiny plane began to approach. With one pass-by, nearing the poles it opened a grappling hook at its rear to release the banner it was towing and instantly hooked onto the stretched cable. At perhaps 80 miles an hour at an 8-foot elevation, the plane stirred up dust as it roared by, seeming close enough to touch. It climbed almost vertically, peeling the banner away from the ground, wobbling a bit as its load became heavy behind it.

It was a fascinating sight. If I had ever thought about it, I would have assumed that the planes would take off with their banners in tow. I asked the field marshal about that. He laughed and said, "They couldn't take off with that heavy banner attached. This way, they just yank it up a little at a time."

Three or four planes repeated this process over and over. It was impossible to walk away from all this activity, the drama of the release-and-catch process making it seem that this time it would be impossible for the pilot to release and catch in one swoop.

"They don't always manage that," the marshal remarked. "Sometimes they have to come around again to catch."

Before long a banner did twist on the way up and had to be dropped in the cornfield. Jack and I hastened to retrieve it. Then it happened again. We weren't allowed to reposition the banners. Placement was not for beginners.

Our planes circled without pause during the game. Some planes, belonging to other companies launched from other sites.

We were incredulous when the game ended. We'd been there for hours that seemed more like minutes.

The marshal thanked us, said we could come again any time. He offered us a ride in one of the planes. I accepted; Jack did not. From the flimsy plane, I could see the ant-like marching band leave the stadium far below. Later I located the roof of our East Lansing house.

We touched down at little Davis Airport on Chandler Road, approximately where today Jimmy's Pub personnel are telling customers about beers on tap.

Jack and I agreed that we would spend at least one afternoon of every future football season playing with the banners. That they wouldn't always be there was unthinkable. If we missed next year, we'd simply go to the next.

Then 9/11 happened. Now, before and after home games, I occasionally hear a tiny plane and look up to see it towing a banner. But there are only a few. No banners fly over the stadium during games. The only noise around the cleared field on the hill is the chirping of birds.

Now we are safe. The question is, from what?

Whiter than White

*I*t's a summer Monday morning in East Lansing, Michigan. The year is 1944, when Monday morning means only one thing – get that laundry out on the line!

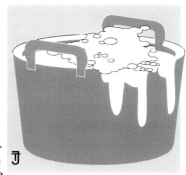

Everyone pretends it isn't a race, but believe me, it is. Radio commercials tell of the "whiter than white" items pegged out by Mrs. Brown, while laundry-impaired Mrs. Green must concede that her grayish dish towels just don't make the grade (undies aren't mentioned on the radio in the '40s). In case Mrs. Green isn't already devastated, the commercial says that because of this new miracle soap, Mrs. Brown beat her by a good 32 ½ minutes, emerging from her basement with a basket of wet clothes at 7:37. Mrs. Brown's pristine sheets hit the line minutes later, at 7:40, to be exact.

In East Lansing I wake with the odor of Fels Naptha soap flakes in my nostrils, reminding me that it's Monday. Though I am only twelve years old I know that I'm a member of Team Laundry, like it or not. And while "Rinso White, Rinso Bright" may be the watchword in other households, we Hoffers don't fall for that stuff. Fels Naptha has a serious smell; no sissy perfumed soaps for us; we'll stick with Fels, even though its thick, sticky flakes glob together if you dump them all in the water at once. Delicate sprinkling techniques must be employed. Detergents slumber undiscovered somewhere in the future.

In our basement Mother has begun the assault. Two stationary molded concrete tubs hold rinse water. A movable tub, complete with a new-fangled electric-powered agitator, yanks sheets and pillow cases mercilessly about in water so hot that we have to hook things out with a shortened broom handle until it cools a bit.

Rotating among the three tubs is my favorite machine, the wringer. After the wash cycle, its length determined by the Chief of Operations, Luella Hoffer, the sheets and towels are cranked through the wringer into Rinse One, swished about and then wrung into Rinse Two.

When Mother isn't looking I delight in swooping an open, wet pillowcase until it balloons, then putting it through the wringer open end first, so the air trapped within makes a delicious sizzling sound as seams threaten to burst.

If Mother is not vigilant, I can do a pillow case this way after each step – three times in all. Mother feels this is too hard on the pillowcases. I simply don't care.

The cleanest stuff goes first – sheets and towels, followed by underwear, outerwear, dirty play and work clothes and finally, rags. Sometimes it's necessary to change the wash water, but on good days we can make it through with one tub-full, even though the water is sudsless and tepid by the time we get to the last items.

I help Mother lug the first load of wet sheets and towels up the basement stairs and out to the back yard. They're very heavy in the galvanized tub. Outside my father has stretched lines from garage to house, back again to the house and over to the huge elm tree. The first sheet, folded double over the line, is hung at 8:10 in the morning. Not bad. Mrs. Brillant has beaten us, but she has only a few things on her line. Other neighbors are probably still filling their tubs.

Warily, we try to analyze the gathering clouds. If it rains, everything will have to dry in the basement as it does in the winter. Laundry dried inside lacks the unmatched fresh smell of the outdoors. I happily haul the laundry up the stairs and out, risking a mad dash to get it in, should we have serious rain.

Heavy items weigh the clothesline down; sheets might drag on the ground. Not to worry, we have notched poles to prop the line.These work perfectly unless we get unusually forceful, un-Michigan-like wind.

We're done by noon. This afternoon we'll need to boil up some starch, dip shirt collars and such, then sprinkle and roll items to be ready for Tuesday's ironing.

The Chief of Operations and I share a sense of well-being. We've done it again. Despite my pillow case folly, we've had a few laughs and shared some secrets. (I think I was the only one who shared, but at twelve I didn't really notice that fact.)

I am part of the team. I will be part of it again on Tuesday when I help iron, and on Saturday when I try to con my mother into chatting so I won't have to dust.

Looking back I see that in those days I knew my place in the world. I was needed. There was satisfaction in a job completed. This knowledge has turned out to be a priceless gift, one that I draw on almost every day.

It is a gift that I would wish for all children, today and for many years to come.

Please Fence Me In

*I*n my life, and probably in most of our lives, boundaries and rules play a big part. The severest test of setting rules and boundaries is parenting. Children begin testing limits at around age two. And I've seen no evidence that they ever give it up. The two year-old makes the happy discovery that he's a separate person from mom and dad. So when they say, "Come here," he runs in the opposite direction. What joy! What adventure!

The adventure continues, with age-appropriate revisions, until adulthood. Then we have to set our own boundaries, a genuine struggle at times.

Most of my working life was in teaching. One story I heard at a workshop made a big impression on me. The speaker drew a little square on the bulletin board. He said, "This is a brand new elementary school. Where do you think the children play during recess?"

After a few guesses from the audience he drew many dots, all close to the building. The children played there, feeling secure next to their school.

Then the speaker drew a large square around the small one. "This is a fence," he said. "Where do you think the children play now that the fence is up?"

We all knew. They played all over the yard, in the farthest corners of the fenced area. Why? Because they felt secure knowing where the boundaries were.

Years later, at Los Angeles County Schools, I taught teens locked up in county juvenile prisons. I did this for 16 years.

One of my first discoveries was that almost all of the teens were hoping someone would put a stop to their behavior. They didn't say this in so many words, but it was clear they had lost control of their lives and in their ability to find a comfortable place to be.

Before they got to us they had been in court at least three times and they were ready for structure. They liked feeling safe, having three meals a day, being away from drugs and gangs, even going to school. They didn't express their personal struggles as right and wrong, but they were tired of being bad. They needed help to be good. They needed boundaries.

Many adult prisoners are the same. They need someone to tell them what to do, when and how. They can't control their lives so their method of handling problems is to mess up and get locked up again, and again.

When children become teens, many will argue, scream, rage and demand trust and freedom even when they know full well that what they are asking for is not in their own best interest. Doesn't matter, they still want the freedom to choose any darn thing they want to do. As the argument escalates they become increasingly convinced that this is what they really, really want. It's hard for parents to see that way down deep the teenager needs help controlling problems of peer pressure. He wants that fence around the school. He really doesn't want to go unarmed into unknown territory. And he can't or won't acknowledge that he needs help.

It is difficult for the parent to hold the line in the face of over-whelming evidence that "everybody does it," that so-and-so's parents aren't home during parties, that your kid will look like a hopeless dweeb if he or she can't do – whatever.

Many years ago my sister's 16-year-old daughter met a boy in Bermuda when she and her mother were there on a vacation. The boy, who was much older, lived in Los Angeles. The daughter wanted to visit him there. She insisted. Life wasn't worth living if she didn't get to go. The battle raged for days.

Finally my sister, exhausted, threw the savings passbook on the living room floor between them and screamed, "Take it! Take the money. Go! Go! I can't do this any more!"

Her daughter looked startled, met her mother's eyes for the first time in days and gently said, "Mom? You really don't want me to go?" It was as if she'd heard it for the first time.

She didn't go.

When I was a very immature 19, a college student living at home, I dated a boy who began to approach me in uncomfortable ways. He wanted me to marry him and move to a trailer near Detroit. He pressured me sexually with all the cliches familiar to girls who have been around a while. I hadn't heard them. I didn't know what to think. I was seriously over my head.

Finally I resorted to the only support system I knew. I sat down opposite my father in the living room and said, "Dad, I want to get married, move to Detroit and live in a trailer."

My father held my gaze for a few seconds, then quietly said, "Well, you aren't going to do that."

"You won't let me?"

"No. You won't get married, not now."

"Okay."

When the boy called later I said, "I can't marry you. My father won't let me."

The boy tried a few more times, but my fence was securely in place and he finally gave up.

One foggy morning in Los Angeles when my son was about 15 years old, I awoke at around five a.m., doubtless because of some built-in mother radar. I looked in his room. Empty. I went out the front door to check on the situation, just in time to meet him tiptoeing around the corner of the house from the back yard.

"Where exactly do you think you're going?"

I don't remember what he said, but he didn't go. Thirty or so years later he told me that some rather unsavory kids at school were going to pick him up that morning to go to the beach. There would be pot smoking, along with other questionable activities. He really didn't feel comfortable about the arrangement, but he didn't know how to get out of it.

"You probably turned my high school life around that morning," he told me. "I was actually relieved, 'though I didn't realize it at the time"

Perhaps I'm being a bit too vehement, here, but over the years I have developed a kind of mantra: Your children want you to be in control. There will be absolutely no evidence of this, in fact there will be much evidence to the contrary. But the world is a scary place and they need to know that a fence is in place.

What To Do?

She missed us by inches, turning left in our path. She might have been upset. A new love gone south? An imagined insult? Struggling to overcome some demon?

Had I been able, I would have questioned her. What made her fly around that corner, oblivious or defiant of the stop sign? We were just two old married people, almost home from an extremely modest dinner at Arbys. Our

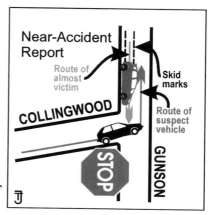

autopsies would have shown only French dip recently entering our dark inside spaces. No drugs, no alcohol. Old coots.

"Snippy" there in her rogue car, young thing with a long blonde ponytail, a college student, perhaps – she would have created such a mess! How dare she? What if . . . what if? What would become of our lives, our house, our cats? I wasn't done with things. Been meaning to leave instructions about the stuff of our lives.

Oh, sure, I should have taken care of these things. But at bottom that would mean lots of hard-nosed getting rid of items that surely no one else would want, then trying to decide who would treasure the remainder. There would be sticky notes, lists.

The real bottom line, though, the true reason for my inaction, is dealing with the idea of my death.

My death. I've died small deaths in my lifetime. The death of my first marriage, the tiny crack, the rift, the chasm that became a canyon. Horrible, irreparable. The death of my second husband, a sudden loss of meaning in my life, the slow, painful rebuilding of the person that I had been before.

Now, complacent, happy, two of us grabbing a bite at Arbys with the gentle, comfortable knowing that everything is okay. No rift, no canyon, no cancer, nothing much to threaten us.

The Snippys of the world could change all that in seconds. Create another death. Mine. Ours.

What to do?

In the moment, I leaned on my horn. She barely noticed.

Limberlost Lost

During my childhood in East Lansing, Michigan in the 1930s and '40s, Burcham Woods was a wondrous playground. It stretched mostly undisturbed north of Burcham Drive all the way to "the highway" (Saginaw Street) – the main route from Lansing to the city of Saginaw and beyond.

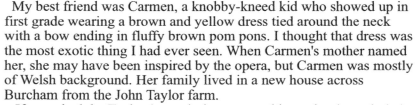

Burcham was only a mile long in those days. There were white-painted frame houses at one end and scattered houses and farm land at the other. On the south side of the street, new platted lots extended to what was the East Lansing city limit.

We children could wander unrestrained in any direction. No one worried about lawsuits and scary strangers. Most doors went unlocked, at least during daylight hours.

My best friend was Carmen, a knobby-kneed kid who showed up in first grade wearing a brown and yellow dress tied around the neck with a bow ending in fluffy brown pom pons. I thought that dress was the most exotic thing I had ever seen. When Carmen's mother named her, she may have been inspired by the opera, but Carmen was mostly of Welsh background. Her family lived in a new house across Burcham from the John Taylor farm.

If we asked the Taylors' permission, we could wander through their cherry orchard, cross their unused fields and explore their woods as much as we liked. On occasion, if Mrs. Taylor said the cherries were ripe enough to eat we gorged ourselves, incurring the predictable stomach ache.

Carmen had a colossal imagination and read voraciously. She could turn the winter skeleton of a tree into a monstrous ghost, a small pond into a quicksand-filled horror.

We didn't know it at the time, but Burcham Woods contained many native hardwoods that the next generations would try mightily to save.

We saw only an immense playground complete with wild flowers of all kinds, a large pond (which we named Taylor's Pond), animal burrows, faint foot paths and, and, deep in the center, a dimly-lit swamp crowded with deadfall. Huge surrounding trees protected the swamp year-round.

I will always remember the day we discovered that brooding, moss-grown swamp. Frightened, we spoke in whispers, digging our fingernails into each other's arms. What a place of mystery! It was so quiet that we could almost hear our hair stand on end. Surely the swamp was as old as the planet on which we stood. This was a new idea to us, and we embellished it with all the fervor of our ten-year-old imaginations.

We played "Girl of the Limberlost," based on a story by Gene Stratton Porter of a girl who grew up near the huge Limberlost swamp in Indiana. We had many a near-disaster while playing Limberlost, rescuing each other from quicksand, from being pinned under falling logs, from wolves and other life-threatening situations.

One day when we were near our deliciously frightening swamp, a man walked toward us, saying we were trespassing on his private land. We apologized, of course, but we weren't lacking in feminine wiles – not at that age anyway. We asked him where he lived. He said on Burcham. We asked if it would be okay for us to play in his woods if we inquired at his house first. He agreed and we always asked.

We worked the woods winter and summer. In winter we could slide on the ice at Taylor's Pond, then build an igloo on the bank and track animal prints in nearby glades. In early spring we gathered jars full of tadpoles. We watched them develop, then returned the survivors to the pond.

On May Day we made little colored-paper cones with pasted-on handles. We canvassed the woods for spring beauties, violets, even trillium, if they were out that early. We arranged the flowers in our paper cones, hung them on the front doors of friendly neighbors, then rang or knocked and dashed to a pre-selected hiding place where we could watch their pleased reactions.

At that time, East Lansing High school was at the end of Burcham Drive facing Abbot Road. It housed grades 7 through 12. Beginning with 7th grade we walked back and forth along Burcham morning, noon and after school.

One particularly spectacular spring day when Carmen and I were in the 11th grade, we were on our way back to school after lunch, but the call of the woods was irresistible. We decided we had to go there, late to school or not. In shaded cool spots we picked wild flowers, reminiscing about our good old days in the woods – pure pleasure. We congratulated ourselves on taking this much-needed detour, declaring it necessary to our mental health.

When we arrived at school – late, of course – we searched out Vice Principal Dorothy Stophlet. "It's such a beautiful day," we told her in a rather well-rehearsed speech. "We just had to go through the woods. We knew that on a perfect spring day like today, the woods would be way more educational for us than any class could possibly be. Here, we picked you these wild flowers." And we presented her with a large bunch of real beauties.

Miss Stophlet played her role. She let us know that we were not in charge of the curriculum, that day or any other. But she left us with the impression that given a choice, she really would have liked to join our small rebellion.

The woods is now only a token strip running past houses, the present high school and a church, ending at the library on Abbot Road. There are still a few native trees. And there is a well-developed path where you can walk and enjoy the woods – to an extent.

But you can't experience the deep stillness that silenced us back then. Our Limberlost swamp, which was about where the back of today's high school sits, is gone. Taylor's pond, just to the north of St. Thomas Aquinas Church and the two homes where we rang the bell to ask permission are also gone.

It is progress, of course, inevitable as our growing old. But we treasure the memories of what once was. And we feel the old person's compulsion to try to share a bit of our experience with those who will never know what they have lost.

# The Coward

Throw some words down.
The group meets tomorrow,
for heaven's sake!

But there's nothing much I want to tell.
Maybe about the . . . no, too personal.
Or the . . . absolutely not!
Perhaps the other day, with Nancy?
Nope, she'd kill me.
A recipe? Oh, please!
My favorite pet? Boring.

As soon as I finish the laundry
and the dishes,
and make that phone call,
then I'll get down to it.
There must be something to write
that won't give me away.

Grandparenting
Smotherless Enjoyment for Relaxed Seniors

*F*or successful grandparenting, my first tip is – raise good children. If you do that, their children will likely respect and value you. How to do this? I haven't a clue.

Raising children is largely a matter of luck, like marrying the right partner. When my daughter's sons were about 5 and 8 years old I stayed with them while their parents took a week-long trip.

One day I congratulated the boys on their excellent, perfect, wonderful behavior (they didn't grasp sarcasm at those ages). The 5 year-old smiled up at me and said, "Well, you have to be good for your grandma!"

It was a great moment.

Grandparents must bear in mind that parents make the rules. Go along with parental rules. Resist the temptation to modify them, or even make them logical. It isn't easy to watch a kid eat a candy bar fifteen minutes before dinner. It's even harder to keep your mouth shut when that same kid at dinner shoves his plate away, making rude remarks about mom's cooking.

Often bed time isn't what it used to be. Parents these days don't always seem to equate being rested with satisfactory daytime performance. You, as a grandparent, can't say anything. Be strong and don't explain anything when you are visiting and have to go to bed an hour before the baby does.

Take your grandchild on a trip, just the two of you, when he or she is around 12 years old. My sister, who more or less survived 14 grand-children, told me to do this. I figured I would give it a try. I've only got three grandchildren, so I thought my health, sanity, and the checkbook could probably survive that many trips.

Following this advice, when my oldest grandson, Carl, was twelve, he and I flew from his Oregon home for three days and three nights in Seattle. We had just rented a car and hit the freeway in five o'clock traffic when he said, "You're a good driver, Grandma." Whoa! I felt like Bobby Unser winning the Indy 500.

Carl, using the AAA book, guided us to the correct off ramp, where he said, "Go to (a five-digit address) on this street." I noticed that we were in the 300 block. The address he gave me must have been in the middle of Puget Sound. Suddenly he cried, "Here it is!" and Bobby Unser made a quick right into the parking lot.

At the desk, I said to the attendant, "Your address is wrong in the AAA book," and I gave him the number.

The somewhat sardonic reply to this was, "Ma'am. That is our zip code."

Oh.

In the elevator Carl and I began to giggle about a motel in Puget Sound.

Things went uphill from there. He was always navigator. He learned a lot about map reading in those three days, especially when, on our way from dinner to the motel one night, we got onto a road that eventually became parallel ruts heading into a swamp. Were we scared or upset? Heck, no, we were invincible. We were pals.

I lived 2500 miles from my grandsons, so baking cookies and dyeing Easter eggs together was pretty much out of the question. E-mail was a good way of keeping in touch, but I found that replies were few.

The phone seemed to be the best option, involving a captive audience. As the boys got older, the conversations became easier, occasionally actually yielding information about their lives. But as they approached their teen years, there seemed to be a reversion to the earlier days of, "Yeah. Nope. Not lately. Maybe." At that age it's called self-protection.

Still, it's important to follow the advice my own father gave me when I was raising my family: Keep those lines of communication open.

If parenting (and grandparenting) can be distilled into one sentence, it seems to me that would be the one. It was true then, and it is true now.

The best part of grandparenting is that you're not responsible for how the kids develop. If you are lucky enough not to be forced by circumstances to be the primary care giver, you've already done your hard parenting work. You are in a position to sit back and watch without undue worry. Whatever happens, it isn't your fault. As a parent, I used to fret a lot about the correct way to handle problems. As a grandparent, I can forget all that and maintain my own mental rating scale: thumbs up for some parental decisions; thumbs down for others.

I'm sure there are many grandparenting tips out there, but these pretty much sum up what I know on the subject. I hope I'll be around long enough to find out how my grandchildren turn out. But then, I don't even know yet how I will turn out.

My primary wish is that when I get to the end of the line, my grandchildren will remember with pleasure the parts of the ride that we were fortunate enough to take together.

Summer Condensed

I once wrote about our expectations of summer - lounging in the hammock with a fresh-squeezed lemonade, reading trashy novels.

Doesn't happen, I said. Before we know it summer is over and we were too busy to lounge or read, almost too busy to notice summer.

A new theory has evolved in my mind: Maybe we can do summer in 30-second segments. Perhaps it's possible to program the mind, to train it to be aware. After all, we can train our muscles, sometimes with amazing results. Why not the brain?

For example, running very late, you park in front of the grocery store. The sun is already setting and you are finally shopping for dinner. Mad rush.

But hold it.

The sunset is at least a ten. Spectacular. You delay 30 seconds to enjoy its vibrant swirls before rushing into the store. You draw a deep breath and begin to feel deep inside that it isn't all about the clock, about dinner.

You've had a sunset, darn it - summer inside you, just waiting to come alive.

On the other end of the day, as early morning light begins to intrude on your dreams, you become aware of bird calls, surprisingly loud, since it's that magic early summer time between furnace and air conditioning when bedroom windows are open. The fresh breeze bears the sound of a train whistle, usually distant, but this morning comfortingly close by. You take your time, lying still, holding sleep in one hand, summer in the other.

Or while weeding frantically along the front sidewalk, you are mentally cataloging all the things you need to do before the in-laws arrive for a week's stay. Can't have weeds anywhere, especially here by the front walk.

But, oh, look! Can it be? A trillium, right here next to the sidewalk. Doesn't the silly thing know it's late in the season for this, that it is endangered?

You rock back on your heels, appreciating it for just 30 seconds. If you wanted it to grow there, it would refuse. Only thing to do now is enjoy summer's little gift.

You carry your morning coffee outside. You watch, listen, check the clouds. A soft, moist breeze touches your face. Is this a mini vacation? No, but perhaps it is an easing of tension; you are looking at clouds instead of a cluttered sink.

Do you know how many people in the world don't have fireflies? I lived in California for 45 years. That's a long time without fireflies. The only compensation was to see my children's enchantment with them when we came to Michigan for a visit. How many fireflies can we see in just 30 seconds? Females winking in the bushes, males circulating, blinking, "Hey, baby!" Rather like a singles bar without the noise.

Thirty seconds might not be quite enough for firefly watching, but if you take along something with ice cubes tinkling in the glass, it is a vacation. No noise, no commercials, just summer in the yard.

Drive with the windows down. If you're a passenger, close your eyes. Try to guess what is around you, taking clues from the various smells. Freshly mown golf course. Corn beginning to tassel out. Newly plowed field. Aromas of the season.

If you must have action, go to an ice cream store on a stifling summer night. The first lick is summer distilled. No one in the store looks even remotely discontented. You have all broken the routine and acknowledged summer, deliciously.

If you use the 30-second method, when September arrives you have an odds-on chance of knowing that summer happened. It has called to you and you have trained your brain to notice and enjoy.

All that remains is to keep noticing.

Summer certainly has its charms.

But fall is almost around the comer. And it's quite beguiling, too.

Sorting it Out

Our grandson Ethan was born in January 2007, my husband Jack's first grandchild. I have three grandsons, but they are teens and twenties people now. So little Ethan was, and continues to be, a miracle.

On an October evening in 2008 we took Ethan, along with his mom and dad, out to dinner. We called it dinner, but it was more like physical education for 17-month olds.

At that age children are very clear about their wants and needs. Ethan did not want to sit. There's a whole world out there, you know, and when you haven't sorted it all out, you want to get started. It's a driving need.

When we were first seated he was busy with tortilla chips. That worked well with our idea of what we were doing. But chips have only so much to offer. Ethan needed to move, to perfect his walking. To run faster and faster.

We were in a back corner of the restaurant, empty at an early hour, so opportunities were nearly limitless. He checked the strength of the walls by slapping them repeatedly. Then he investigated the sturdiness of various chairs. He was peeled away from several place settings, redirected toward apple juice and cheese quesadilla. He had no interest in either.

Mom took the first turn with him, out the door, up and down the sidewalk. He learned that cracks in the concrete cannot be pried up with a finger. She shared that with us.

Next was Dad who pointed out structural features of the building and various cars in the parking lot. Ethan seemed to prefer the red cars.

Grandpa Jack volunteered next. Through the window we saw Jack and Ethan walking sedately up and down, probably discussing world events and the intricacies of weeds next to the sidewalk.

My turn at last! Ethan and I struck out across the driveway. He soon spotted a grassy slope, small and rather steep. Down we went, holding hands. He giggled all the way down and immediately needed to climb back up. Repetition is very, very popular at his age, so we repeated the adventure three or four times.

After one successful descent, we picked some spectacular Queen Anne's Lace for Mom. We had to be sure it was bug free. "These blossoms seem to be a favorite hiding place for bugs," I said. Ethan agreed.

Just as we turned around in preparation for the final ascent, something wonderful happened. The automatic sprinklers came on. They rose up from the ground and began their stately, deliberate arc, right to left and back again. Instant Disneyland! We bobbed, wove, laughed and swatted drops, all the while complimenting ourselves on finding this previously hidden excitement.

Mom loved the flowers. Slightly damp but happy, Ethan exchanged a few high-fives with Dad.

What joy! At 17 months everything is new, exciting, just waiting to be experienced.

And so it was at age 76.

The good news is that I still haven't sorted it all out.

Dolly

Dolly entered our lives on a long-ago Christmas when our son, Andy was three and our daughter, Erica, one. We helped her open the package, enjoying her delight at seeing the aristocratic, lovely doll. A wreath of blonde hair framed the classic features, accented by clear azure eyes. The doll wore a frilly christening dress. Arms and legs of a soft plastic-like material were attached to her cuddly cotton body, the legs ending in feet clad in white shoes with tiny, real snaps on the straps.

She wasn't Dolly then. We thought that she would be hugged, cherished and given a name like Stephanie or Georgina by an older Erica. But we reckoned without Andy.

Andy preempted her from the start, which for the doll was tantamount to being rocketed from pink nursery to street gang.

Technically she remained Erica's, but within days her hairdo became a startling topknot, sticking straight up like the convenient carrying handle that it was. She swung in wide arcs, tethered only by her hair. The christening dress began to look like the gowns of fallen nobility. The shoes disappeared. And her name became Dolly.

One-year-olds are pretty compliant. Erica made no protest. She didn't seem overly fond of dolls anyway, preferring teddy bears and more user-friendly toys.

As Andy passed through early childhood, Dolly played an important role in his life. She stamped her plastic feet and refused to eat what Andy didn't like. She expressed opinions and emotions that Andy wouldn't dare express. She even experimented with bad words on occasion. At times she flew through the air, aimed at offending family members or other critical targets. Sometimes she flew for the simple joy of flying. Often she was grounded, or shelved, as it were.

The christening dress became a distant memory. Dolly's body began to wear out. Her left foot turned backward, dangling pitifully, probably because of too many unfortunate landings. Her face was ink-stained, her hair mostly gone. Scrubbing her angelic face with cleanser made me feel as if I were hurting her. She had become as real to our family as the Velveteen Rabbit.

Since she was such an important family member, we couldn't ignore her unsightliness. I found some fake fur tiger-striped fabric in the rag bag. It certainly seemed to fit Dolly's personality. I made pants and a tunic from the tiger material.

Our beloved baby sitter, Grandma U., saddened by the bald head and open pores where hair had been, arrived one day with bright blue and red yarns. She crocheted a blue bonnet with red edging and a blue sweater, also with red edging. The ensemble made quite a fashion statement, over the tiger suit and all.

Our family took many long car trips. Dolly misbehaved a lot on these trips. She demanded snacks, refused to close her eyes and rest, complained about staying in the car while the family went to Dairy Queen. Occasionally Dolly would noisily beat up on other toys, destroy Etch-a-Sketch designs and pull Color Forms off the car windows.

Finally the inevitable happened. We banned Dolly from car trips. Flying through a bedroom is one thing; doing a kamakaze dive past the driver's head, quite another. By this time Andy and Erica were older and occasionally they worked together at making Dolly obnoxious and antisocial. A new game developed – smuggling Dolly on board.

"No Dolly, no exceptions," we said while stuffing ice chests and duffel bags into the car. Things would be relatively peaceful until along about Day Three when a ghastly, ink-stained, blue-bonneted head would appear over the back edge of the front seat.

"HI!" Dolly would croak in her trademark squeaky voice, causing Andy and Erica to erupt with wild glee. Dolly had really put one over on us – again. Thankfully, by those years Dolly didn't seem to feel the need to act out quite so often.

When Andy was sixteen and Erica thirteen, a wrapped shoe box under the Christmas tree bore the tag, "To Erica from Andy." For the second time in her life, Erica unwrapped her doll. She lovingly cuddled the now aged, grotesque, arthritic Dolly.

Watching them, we felt the rush of time; how quickly Dolly's reign had come and gone. She had outlived her role in the family. She had lost her power. Her wide open sky-blue eyes contemplated her future. They were the only thing about her that hadn't changed.

Everything else was different.

Now, many years later, Dolly lives in an old pillowcase in a closet in Bend, Oregon. Even though Andy gave her back to Erica, Dolly is still at Andy's house. Andy, age 43 at this writing, periodically decides to clean house and the pillowcase hovers over a trash can. But his fingers refuse to release their grip and Dolly returns to her condominium in the closet. Perhaps throwing her out feels too much like betrayal.

Remembrance of old love sometimes doesn't die easily.

Learning to Drive
East Lansing, Michigan, 1945

*A*s my 14th birthday approached, it was time for me to learn to drive. In those days, driver's licenses were issued to 14 year-olds. Driver training classes were far in the future, so the job of teaching fell to my parents, a demanding task, complicated by the fact that they had launched my brother into the driving world only two years earlier. I have never met a parent who looked forward to teaching a kid to drive. Most likely that is why driver training eventually was foisted off on the schools.

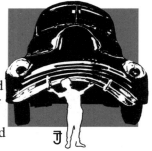

My father was appointed Main Instructor, which says something about the cleverness of my mother. Saturdays or Sundays Dad and I practiced in Michigan State College parking lots, empty on weekends back then.

Automatic transmissions were far in the future. Learning to coordinate clutch, accelerator and brake was daunting. Dad and I rode (well, more like slammed and jounced) through abrupt stalls, jerky starts and horrible grindings of gears. Seeing his arms braced on the dash prior to a stop didn't add anything to my confidence. (Seat belts were un-dreamed-of then.) He was down-right valiant, trying to disguise his obvious terror.

To me, my beginning lessons seemed very short. "Time to head home," he would announce with an animated voice I hadn't heard during the lesson.

"Aw, Dad, we just got here. Let me try that first-to-second gear thing one more time. I know I can do it this time. Please." I would usually be granted another opportunity to coax the protesting floor-mounted shift lever from first to second.

"Be sure the clutch is ALL the way in!" Dad would yell as gears met in unintended ways.

After I got past tooth-rattling stops and screaming gear changes, we moved on to backing up, pretend parallel parking and signaling for turns and stops. For turns, all drivers relied on hand signals. (Steering-wheel turn signals came much later.) These were done by sticking one's arm out of the open driver's-side window, especially fun on sub zero winter days or in heavy rainstorms. When the left arm was bent up 90 degrees it told the driver behind you: "I'm going to turn right." Straight out: "I'm turning left here." And straight down, palm to the rear: "I'm going to stop now."

When I had the basics more or less in place, Dad and I ventured onto the open road, Farm Lane, far south near the railroad tracks, where there were no buildings, no crossroads and very little traffic. In my mind, however, the southernmost railroad crossing will forever be synonymous with terror.

One Sunday afternoon when we were inches from the tracks, Dad suddenly yelled, "Look out!" I slammed on the brakes, sending him sprawling. The engine stalled, of course.

Squeezing my eyes shut, I braced for the impending crash, but nothing happened.

Climbing back onto the seat, Dad, somewhat abashed, said, "There are some terrible bumps there."

Sixty years later, I would still smile as I crossed those tracks, slowing for the great-grandchildren of those same bumps.

One pivotal day Dad and I ventured all the way to downtown East Lansing to practice parallel parking. For this, timing was everything. You had to give plenty of warning to the person behind you. Tailgating was far less prevalent then. Drivers needed a lot of lead time because hand signals were much more difficult to see than today's turn signals.

Consider: in a driving rainstorm you locate a parking space directly in front of The Mar-Jo Shop (ladies' dresses). You crank the window open (no such thing as automatic windows then, either), stick out your left arm and point it down to indicate a stop. In the rear view mirror you see a rapidly approaching 1938 Oldsmobile. You wiggle your arm; pump it vigorously. Finally the driver rolls to a stop, having realized you are attempting to communicate.

Then comes the embarrassing business of getting parked. You have to back in (unless there are several vacancies and you can swoop in straight ahead). Perilously close to the car parked on your right, you turn your steering wheel hard to the right and point the back of your car toward the space. You back at an angle until your left rear fender is about half a car's width into the center of the space. Then you crank the wheel to the left and continue backing while making sure the front end of your car doesn't hit the one in front and that you don't slam into the one in back. If all goes well you straighten the wheel and settle into the space. If not, you have to start over, and the person driving the 1938 Oldsmobile is not at all happy with this decision.

Beginning drivers – even intermediate ones – often required several passes before they either succeeded or gave up. Parallel parking is the same today, except that drivers hardly ever need to do it. Streets where parking is in demand are too busy to allow cars to stop and wait for a driver to struggle into a space. Off-street parking is the norm today.

But, without question, the graduate degree in driving when I learned was the dreaded Starting On A Hill maneuver. Automatic transmissions have simplified this operation, but in the days of separate clutch, brake and accelerator pedals, starting uphill was a challenge, requiring a more relaxed teacher than my father ever could be. He had an irrational fear that a stall would cause us to plunge backward down the hill like a runaway freight car, mindlessly crushing everything and everyone in its path.

To start on a hill required intense concentration: You put your left foot on the clutch, your right on the brake, pushed the starter button, then swiveled your right foot to control both the brake and the accelerator.

When you felt you had sufficient RPMs (whatever those were), you eased off on the clutch and brake while increasing pressure on the accelerator.

If all went well you started up the hill as planned. You had to keep up the momentum so the engine wouldn't stall.

I failed many times before earning this advanced degree. My father added lots of gray to the fringe above his ears.

After I had my license our family had four drivers and one car. The neighbors used to tease us about our numerous runs in and out of the driveway. My parents were very tolerant in accommodating our eagerness to drive the car.

As a teen I had my share of scrapes, once nearly taking out a telephone pole at the corner of Fern and Forest (I still smile when I pass that corner, too) and another time requiring a late-night tow on the golf course at Walnut Hills. (Don't ask.)

At age 22, I married and moved to Los Angeles. Thanks to Dad, I was able to hone my killer driving instincts and manage quite well in the car-infested streets of that pre-freeway city.

Now, living again in my home town, I have forgiven my father for the railroad crossing incident. Overall, he did a fine job. I consider myself a good driver, though a bit heavy on Los Angeles survival techniques. If I get to heaven and find there are cars, I'll take Dad for a spin. But I'll be searching out bumpy railroad crossings. Even though I have long since forgiven him, I'd like to shout "Look out!" at the exact moment tire meets track.

Then we both could smile.

Stormy Morning

Dawn has arrived. That is, it's on its way, probably passing somewhere near Erie, Pennsylvania, at the moment. Snuggled in our bed, my husband, Jack, and I are unaware. We aren't terribly excited about dawn.

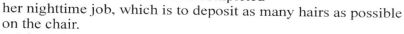

But our cat, Storm, is brilliant when it comes to dawn. And she just cannot wait to share.

I hear a "thump" as she jumps down from her sleeping spot, my computer chair across the room. She has completed her nighttime job, which is to deposit as many hairs as possible on the chair.

After a jump up to the cedar chest at the foot of the bed and another to the bed, she begins a march toward our heads, placing her feet with all the subtlety of a 7.9 earthquake. Storm is not small – eighteen pounds standing, fifty five pounds when we pick her up. Picking her up has to be her idea, never ours.

She taps me on the shoulder. I shrug her off and pull the covers over my head. She pushes them aside to examine my left nostril. It seems to satisfy, so she moves to Jack's chest in order to listen to his heartbeat. Finding us alive is a joyous thing. Her deafening purr tells us so.

Because she is a cat, her definition of an alive human is, "able to dispense food."

I've explained to her about weekends, suggesting she might enjoy sleeping in. I've promised her extra rations if she can stay in her chair for, say, an extra thirty minutes. She refuses to listen. Listening to humans would be a breach of cat ethics.

The upside is that we will never have to buy an alarm clock, and maybe that's okay.

Cats don't have to be wound up or connected to an electrical outlet.

Over the life of a cat that could save us enough to buy, say, 20 pounds of cat chow. A superior brand, even.

As I write this, Storm sits nearby purring loudly, no doubt delighted that I have finally figured out who is in charge here.

Good Wishes for "Bad Boys"

*B*ad boys. In the 1980s and
'90s, Challenger Memorial
Youth Center in Lancaster,
California, where I taught,
housed and taught 600 of them.
Challenger was a Los Angeles
County Probation Department
facility. Chances are that a
young man had seen the inside
of a juvenile court two, three,

or even four times before he found himself incarcerated at
Challenger. This facility was not the law's first line of defense;
more like the last before the California Youth Authority, the place
where the really bad boys went.

Our boys were a mix of many ethnic and racial persuasions,
some tattooed in truly incredible ways, some relatively unmarked,
some products of mean streets, others of too much alcohol or
drugs. Car thieves. Gangbangers. Probation violaters. Drug
dealers. Tough. Vulnerable.

Having parents who cared and worried. Having no parents.
Going to make sure their little brothers didn't end up there.
Going to take care of that baby their girlfriend was about to have,
or already had. Going to get off drugs or alcohol. Never coming
back.

Uncle at Folsom Prison. Mom at Sybil Brand, a women's
detention facility.

There was, however, one quality that nearly all of our clients
had in common: They were expert manipulators. They could size
up a situation in a nanosecond. They played it any way they
wanted, any time they wanted. As a teacher, I saw and even
admired this skill many times.

Jorge (not his real name) was nearing expert status in manipulation. He had clear, twinkling eyes and a sense of humor,
something that was hard to find in this population. His smile
would melt the most hardened heart. He had learned to tilt his
head a certain way and use a particular squeaky-falsetto voice to
cadge and plead for whatever he needed.

Not wanted. Needed.

He asked how you were feeling that day. He admired something
you were wearing. He told the other boys to behave, have respect.

Jorge was more than a little hyperactive. He could be standing up, walking to the pencil sharpener and when asked to sit down, tell you sincerely that he was sitting down, and that was his honest perception.

A student might tell you that he was picked up for violation of probation while just walking down the street. Upon questioning, he might come up with the fact that he had a 12-pack under each arm, and it was 12:30 in the morning, but, man, he was just walking down the street!

To return to Jorge, his father was absent but sent money to the family, lots and lots of money. You got a "drug dealer" feeling. Jorge lived with his mother and sisters. He was going to take care of his mom when he got out, even though he was only 15. He was going to set a good example for his younger siblings. So, what did he need? Maybe a mom. Maybe a dad.

One day Jorge was talking to a classmate, unaware that I was listening. The discussion was about school on the "outs." His classmate said that he really hated to go to school on the "outs" – didn't go, in fact, which was the case with many others in the room.

But Jorge said that he loved school on the outs. It was great. Especially, he said, on the days when his mother was home. "All whacked out."

That was Jorge's reality. But he had survival tools. Maybe he was able to make it.

Then there was another boy, a special-education student. An Individual Educational Plan (IEP) was required for such students. The state mandated a review of this plan every year, involving a special education teacher, parents, classroom teachers and others who were involved with the student, such as speech therapists.

In our camp, a surrogate sometimes acted in lieu of the parent at an IEP conference, perhaps because there was no parent, or because the parent lived too far away to trek the many miles to our desert facility. Maybe the parent's work schedule prevented his coming. Or, she might have chosen to ignore the event.

This particular boy's mother did make it, late and breathless. She told how her car had been totaled in a wreck and she had to rent a car to come from near downtown Los Angeles, the rental costing her $178, excessive in the 1980s.

At lunch the next day when we teachers discussed the story, we were somewhat incredulous: $178 for the car! We speculated that the mother probably didn't have a credit card, so maybe part of the cost would have been a deposit, maybe partially refundable. Maybe she was taken advantage of, since she wanted so badly to come to the conference.

The resource teacher said, "He is really a nice kid." At this, there were some cynical comments around the table. "No, really," she said. "His problems are nearly all because he is special ed, and that is what has gotten him into so much trouble."

He might have been hyperactive, like Jorge, or he was the kind of student who was confused by too much going on around him. If the teacher said, "Open your book to page fifty. Do problems one through twelve. Be sure your columns are straight, and turn in your paper to me when you are finished," some special ed students could be lost after the first instruction. There were myriad reasons why these students might have run-ins with the law, not the least of which could be lack of success in school.

After the resource teacher made her remark about the "nice" kid there was a lull as we at the table pondered the mother who loved her child so much. There was an unexpressed feeling among us: Please let him be successful on the "outs" when he goes home.

Years ago, at another facility where I worked, a social worker talked about the parenting needs of so many among the juvenile offender population. "Everybody needs a parent," she said,"We need someone to give the best Christmas gift, someone who wants to hear about our day at school, someone who can be counted on never to forget our birthday."

One day the social worker was counseling a boy, discussing options for him when he was released. They searched his life situation for grandparents, aunts, older siblings – anyone with whom he could possibly live.

After an exhaustive session, the boy looked at her and said, "Maybe I could go home with you, Kay."

What kind of answers can you give to a bad boy?

Diplomacy

She's a gutsy little cat, looks like a walking birds nest. A stray, she has no name that we know. Our next-door neighbor, Sylvia, provides food and water. During winter she occasionally finds the cat on her back stoop at bedtime. If the cat is there, it means a sub-zero night is on the way, so she opens the door. The cat scurries to the basement and settles in, but demands to go out again long before daylight.

One early evening in late fall, we spotted the stray bathing and grooming in Sylvia's back yard, under the bird feeder. Ears, tail, belly – each had a luxurious turn. It was a slow process, punctuated by long pauses and leisurely stretches.

On a nearby bush lived 40 or so house sparrows. They found it an excellent location, near the feeder and electrically warmed water bowl. This particular evening, 80 or so bird eyes glared at the cat. We knew they were glaring because in order to glare, you have to be rigid, focused, unmoving – not the norm for birds.

One sparrow finally broke ranks and flicked his tail. His meaning was clear, "The cat must go. We require food." Usually the birds move as one in a drifting beige and black cloud, mounting and surrounding the feeder, searching the ground beneath to see if the squirrels have left anything. This was not possible.

Cat!

The birds dispatched a scouting party to swoop over the cat, to remind her of their eminent domain. This was not news to the cat. All along she was well aware that they were there. She yawned, gave her ear a rub, and stretched out for a nap under the feeder.

Finally the birds fled to the top of a nearby Norway pine, where they held a noisy, unruly conference. Indignant cheeps and chirps shattered the evening quiet. They seemed to be having trouble reaching consensus. As darkness fell, the impasse held. We could almost hear tiny bird stomachs rumbling.

Sadly for the birds, it was not going to be a sub-zero night.

Treachery in the Radiation Lab

*I*n February 2004, I am in the fourth of six weeks of daily radiation to prevent recurrence of my breast cancer. Each weekday morning I leave the house at eight to go to Ingham Medical Center for treatment. I had a lumpectomy in November to remove a not-very-scary cancerous mass.

Patients quickly learn the drill. You don't check in at the reception desk, you proceed immediately to the waiting room, pull a key from a locker, and enter a dressing room.

If you're a breast cancer patient you strip to the waist and don a hospital gown. Then you stuff your things into the locker, lock it, and pin the key on your gown with the attached large pin.

Professionals in the radiation lab seem to be tireless in their efforts to make it a pleasant place to be. A young man offers his arm as we march to the radiation area, making me think he'll ask, "Bride's side or groom's side?"

The waiting room is inviting. Besides the usual magazines and upholstered armchairs there's an aquarium and, in the center of every-thing, a large table bearing a very complex jigsaw puzzle.

Appointments are roughly at the same time each day, so you begin to recognize your fellow patients. Today when I arrived a man I hadn't seen previously was finishing the 1,000 piece aquarium puzzle that had been on the table for about five days. "My kids used to steal the last piece and cough it up when we were all done," I said, "just so they could put the very last one in."

"My wife does that," he replied. "Can't trust her at all." After a pause to search out a special piece of angelfish, he continued, stating what is always on the mind and seldom spoken. "We've been fighting this thing since June. This is only our second radiation day. It'll be six weeks. We live an hour away, so we scheduled her for 8:10 in the morning. That way maybe I can make it to work for at least a half day."

I shared my brief history with him and found the fin of clown fish. We were down to four pieces.

When those were in place we discovered one empty spot. We searched the floor, shook the box. No dice.

She came back to the waiting room on crutches, looking wan, but smiling warmly at us.

"We finished the puzzle!" I sang in the familiar "Nya, nya-nya Nya Nya" singsong.

"You did? You couldn't have!" She pawed around in her purse and pulled out the last puzzle piece.

By this time we'd been joined by several others – two women, one wearing a scarf and one a hat and a man leaning heavily on a walker. Almost in unison we cried, "Traitor! Cheat! Rat!" Our laughter rang around the room, enough laughter to push back self-pity and dark thoughts, at least for that moment.

"She must have taken it home with her yesterday," her husband said. "Goes to show that just because they're on crutches, doesn't mean you can trust them."

"I did! I took it home!" she cried, joyously unrepentant.

"Probably can't beat up on her," I observed. "What with the crutches and all."

Her treachery was discussed with much merriment in the radiation room, the adjoining offices and at the nurses' desk.

Tomorrow I'm going to take a computer-generated notice to tape onto the puzzle table:

**<center>Anyone who removes the last puzzle piece
will be prosecuted to the full extent of the law.
Don't even think about it!</center>**

If we don't laugh at that, one thing is for sure – we'll find something else to make each other smile. It's our job, one we all take very seriously.

Fire in the Hole

*O*n an early morning in June 1994, my husband, Russ, heard a snapping noise and dropped to the floor. His cancer-destroyed femur had broken. Surgeons inserted a steel rod to support the bone. When he left the hospital he went to a gritty nursing home for three weeks of rehab. Our worst nightmare was that he would never leave the place. But he did. He had

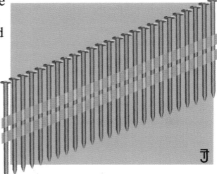

doctor's orders to go home and enjoy life.

Right.

We rented a hospital bed and put it in the family room next to the kitchen. Russ was miserable in our bedroom – claustrophobic, he said. He couldn't bear that too-serene, isolated room, darkened by a patio roof extending over the only window.

From his new bed Russ could see the front door, the kitchen and the back yard. Almost within his reach, an 8-foot sliding glass door led to the patio. The sunny room was perfect for enjoying life.

Right.

Whatever time he had left, it certainly was not enough. Friends brought books, food and murky potions with odd labels. A co-worker loaned us meditation tapes by Bernie Siegel, a famous person, who, it was said, had helped many terminal people. When Russ and I played the first tape, Bernie began to talk of beautiful meadows rimmed with flowers, animals gamboling about. All we could do was cry. Forget that.

"Tell you what," said Russ. "I've been wanting to fix up the patio." The patio that came with the house, rather crudely constructed of brick, stone and concrete, was a step down from the inside floor level.

"Let's get someone over to see about putting a wood deck over this mess," he said. "Same floor level as the house. I could just mosey on out when I wanted to." He could do that, all right, if one can mosey while clinging to a walker or operating a wheel chair.

Several days later, Ralph the carpenter, a cheerful young man, showed up. "Hey, no problem." he said, "I'll have that sucker built in a few days."

Ralph's first challenge was to anchor the new floor in the existing concrete. "I'll rent a hammer gun," he said. "Just shoot some bolts in there. It's basically a rifle with an adaptor You put in a bolt and wham! Won't take any time at all."

The next morning Ralph proudly displayed his lethal weapon. Impressive, we thought. He strutted out, took aim and shouted "Fire in the hole!" That's what people yell when a serious explosion is about to take place.

Click.

Ralph tried it again.

Click.

"Tough sonofagun," grunted Ralph. The clicks went on for some time, Ralph becoming increasingly embarrassed and Russ increasingly frustrated.

Finally Russ sidled out of bed, grabbed his walker, worked his way outside and reached for the gun. "Let me give it a try," he said, panting. He was a ridiculous figure – striped pajama bottoms, flapping shirt, wild hair and wooly slippers, leaning on the walker, aiming the barrel inches from the concrete.

"Fire in the hole!" he called.

Blam!

"I'll be darned," said Ralph.

Can a person leaning on a walker, wearing striped pajamas, swagger? You bet your life.

"That's how it's done, my man," said Russ.

Laughter felt odd. A mix of tragic irony and comic relief loosened our muscles, allowed our lungs to expand and our hearts to feel a stirring very like happiness, if only for a moment.

That day Ralph tried repeatedly to make the infernal thing work. He never succeeded.

But Old Striped Pajamas hit it every time.

Had he not, all three of us would have been heartbroken.

On Deaf Ears

*I*n their columns, Ann Landers and Dear Abby used to say, "Just tell them. Talk it over. Be direct about problems." I've occasionally tried using that approach, but my results are not good, not measurable, as the scientists say.

Back in the 1960s and '70s in California our next door neighbors had a very large white Samoyed dog. Each night after dark they would send Sukie out to do her business on our lawn.

Their lawn was fenced, its tea rose border aphid-free. It being the 1960s, they had that favorite of paranoids, a bomb shelter, buried deep beneath their yard. Apparently they thought dog poop would be out of place in such an unsullied yard, which told us something about what they thought of us. We knew for sure that in an emergency we would never get into that bomb shelter. They would gun us down at the door. People used to discuss things like that back then.

Sukie preferred a spot adjacent to our driveway. Entering and leaving the car, for us, was kind of an adventure.

Finally I decided to put my money on Dear Abby. Over a cup of tea in the neighbor's kitchen I broached the subject.

"Hey, Martha. Sukie's pooping on our lawn every night," I said. How straightforward can you get? I didn't say, "Why is our yard your mutt's bathroom?" I didn't say, "How come you wait until dark to let it sneak into our yard?" I didn't say, "A lot of other dogs now use that spot, thanks to Sukie." I thought I was quite restrained, considering.

"Not Sukie," Martha replied.

"Oh, it's Sukie, all right. I see her every night."

Martha delivered some version of Jack Benny"s celebrated, "W E L L!" and I left her house. Forever, as it turned out.

After that she began to call when there was a rose missing among the thousands in their border; or when my son's band was practicing (loudly, I admit) during the afternoon. (It never practiced at night.)

Ann and Abby told readers that the direct approach promotes instant understanding for both parties. Not peace, maybe, but we certainly know what the other is thinking.

Years ago when a friend's son was about to be married he called her for advice. "What do you really, really think, Mom? About me marrying her, I mean."

"What do I really, really, really think?" she said. "Do you really, really want to know?"

"Yeah. Absolutely."

She took a deep breath and said, "Honestly I'm pretty concerned about her neurotic behavior." She waited for the explosion.

"Oh. That," he said, "That's all over. Used to be a problem. Not anymore."

The wedding, of course, went on as planned.

But not the marriage.

Over the years it has become clear that even when delivered in the most straightforward manner, most advice sails through the eardrum and exits the brain unprocessed.

Years ago I said to my daughter, "Balancing a checkbook is a very good idea, especially before writing a large check."

"Nobody does that," she replied. She has since learned – from the bank, not me.

"Let the baby fuss a bit," I told my son and his wife, six weeks after their son was born. "We used to set the timer for ten minutes at bedtime. After that if you were still unhappy we would come in and see if there was a problem."

After a month or so of sleepless nights, my son called me. "Guess what!" he said, "At the doctor's they gave us this book about babies' sleep problems. It said to let them fuss for a while when you put them down. Mom, it really works!"

Over the years I have spent quite a lot of energy rescuing those who didn't really want to be rescued and advising those who asked for advice, along with quite a few who didn't actually ask. All my efforts ended with identical results – nothing measurable. You'd think I would learn. You'd think I'd ask someone for advice about whether to give advice.

But what would they know?

The President Comes to Town
written in 2008

*T*he summer of 1948 brought a presidential campaign, just as in 2008. I was
about to be a junior in high school,
World War II was over, President Franklin
Roosevelt had died and President Harry
Truman had won the Democratic
nomination.

Harry Truman was coming to Lansing.
This did not generate great excitement
because everyone was sure that he, who
had assumed the office after Roosevelt's death, would never win the
election. Thomas Dewey, born in Owosso, Michigan, was the clear
favorite.

But what the heck! A bunch of us high school kids showed up at the
Pere Marquette Depot in Lansing on a simmering summer morning,
probably in early August. There weren't too many people there, a
respectable crowd, but no stampede.

Truman was to ride through on his private train and pause to talk to
the "folks" from the platform at the back of the last car, just as we
expected. Candidates had been campaigning this way forever, to our
way of thinking.

Waiting for the train, I heard many cynical remarks. "Might as well
see what the guy looks like. It's the only time we're ever gonna see
him."

And, "Talk about being out of touch. That's our Harry!"

"He completely rebuilt the White House, you know. The nerve!"

Our Hoffer family was what then was called "dyed-in-the-wool
Democrats." This made us a distinct minority in East Lansing,
Michigan. Once a back-yard neighbor said to my mother, "Well,
you know, only the reds and the riffraff voted for Roosevelt!" Mom
thought that was pretty funny.

I remember walking to elementary school along about third or fourth
grade. It was an election year. Someone said that the Republican
candidate was going to win, that Roosevelt was done for, and about
time, too. I said nothing, but another kid piped up, "Shut up! Hoffer's
a Democrat." I was bewildered.

Me? I was just a little kid.

During my just-completed sophomore year, one of my classes had
written and performed singing political commercials. We three
Democrats in the class had bravely sung, to the tune of the "Missouri
Waltz,"

"Vote for Harry Truman, let the people have their way. And you won't be sorry on Inauguration Day." Comic relief, perhaps. The applause was anemic.

This hot summer day we heard a throaty whistle and soon the train chugged to a stop, blocking Michigan Avenue. Harry was already on the platform. He looked vibrant and alive, the sun glinting off his glasses. We had probably seen very few, if any, color photographs of the man.

He spoke a bit about specific local issues and mentioned Michigan State College "over there," pointing in the right direction.

But the best part for me was when he was winding down, after maybe ten minutes. He said, "I'd like you to meet my daughter, Margaret." She stepped out, smiled and waved. She was pretty! Margaret did not photograph well, so some in the crowd expressed surprise. "I'll be darned. She's not as homely as I thought."

Margaret, born in 1924, would have been 24 at the time. Not knowing this, I thought that she was younger – maybe 16 or 17.

Not long ago, in 2008, thousands greeted presidential candidate Barack Obama in Lansing. He spoke at the convention center just a few blocks from the depot. Perhaps some in the huge crowd came just because they wanted to get a look at him.

I wonder what they will think as history dictates the outcome of this election? In 1948 the one image that stays with those of us who were around then is of Truman holding a newspaper with the (inexact) headline, "Dewey Defeats Truman!"

Truman is smiling widely. And we all know why.

Pepper the Geriatric Dog

A cockapoo is not a bird. You probably know that. But just in case you don't, it is a cocker-poodle mix – a dog.

Sometime in the early 1980s my husband's ex wife brought Pepper the cockapoo to live with us. Well, not exactly to live with us. Pepper was terminal. Ex-wife Jeanne didn't have the grit to deal with this situation, so she asked her former co-dog owner to take care of the problem. In truth, she left Pepper with us to die.

Jeanne and Pepper lived in West Los Angeles, Russ and I in the canyons between Los Angeles and the Mojave Desert. We were some 70 miles apart but vastly different in climate. Fleas loved West Los Angeles. Its near-the-beach dampness and mild temperatures provided a perfect Eden for them, especially given the availability of a hapless curly-haired host cockapoo.

Our canyon had a desert climate. In the 1980s fleas couldn't tolerate our dryness and seasonal frosts. There were no fleas in the canyon then. Not so now, with many "new" homes with large, irrigated lawns.

When he arrived, Pepper's eyes were milky, making him nearly blind. He was so feeble that he could barely navigate the steps into our house. Our two rambunctious dogs nearly flattened the poor guy when they raced to their dishes at feeding time. Pepper nosed a bit at his dish, then left it to Cody and Kipper, who were doggedly grateful. Sorry.

Pepper began to build up steam. As the fleas expired, his blood count must have soared. Oh, he was no Clark Kent of dogdom, but he essayed the occasional romp with Cody and Kipper. When they tore up and down the driveway he limped along behind, more or less happy, tail swishing tentatively.

Soon his eyes began to clear. He learned to bark again. His appetite increased, much to the disappointment of his compadres.

Around this time Russ and I purchased two acres in the for-real desert near a burg called Pinon Hills. We decided to explore our purchase by camping there for a weekend. Our new acquisition was filled with promise – there would be piped water within months, the road would be paved.

But on this weekend our homestead was indistinguishable from the miles of cactus, sage, sand and Joshua trees that stretched on all sides. We thought we camped on our property, but there was no way to be absolutely sure.

With coyotes and other native critters in mind, we brought along stout chains for our two dogs, but thought Pepper too infirm to leave our sides. We slept soundly in the bed of our truck, the stars almost within reach, comforted by the singing of those stout chains as our big dogs nosed about.

When we awoke, Cody and Kipper greeted us joyously, but there was no Pepper. Poor thing, we thought, must have dragged his tired bones off somewhere to be caught by a coyote. We felt guilty and sad. We agreed we'd never tell Jeanne how it happened.

Along about mid-afternoon, there was a swishing in the brush and in strode a cockapoo. Not Pepper, we thought. This dog was the Clark Kent of dogdom. His eyes shone, his coat was sleek; he strutted. He was bragging!

"Pepper?" we said, unbelieving.

"Most certainly," he replied, "You were expecting maybe some kind of wimp dog?" Of course he didn't actually say it. Cockapoos are gifted at body language.

After a moment, I ventured a guess. "Russ," I asked, "was Pepper ever neutered?"

"Matter of fact, no," he replied.

"Pepper? What have you been doing?" Russ asked.

"What do you think?" said Pepper.

Pepper lasted long enough to see the road paved and the piped water come in. In fact, he enjoyed five more years with us. He was mildly upset that one of our first acts was to erect a chain link fence. He approved of the mobile home we put on the property. He gave Cody and Kipper the occasional run for their money.

But best of all, Pepper never divulged to Cody and Kipper the fact that they had been neutered.

Up to Speed

*T*ext. Tweet. Blog. Why are all these people so busy? As a woman of some age, I sometimes feel painfully out of the loop. Now and then I wish I could pick up the phone, find Ernestine the operator and ask her to connect my party. It's hard for those of us who started

with five-digit phone numbers to enter the mobile information era.

This became clear in April 2010 at the Philadelphia airport when husband, Jack, and I met daughter Erica and her husband, Randy who flew in from Walla Walla, Washington. We drove to Cape May, New Jersey to celebrate their son Keith's graduation from the Coast Guard Training Center.

After our four days together, Jack and I planned to drive the rental car on to Gaithersburg, Maryland, to visit his brother. Erica decided that we needed a GPS thingy for the trip.

"It sits on the dash," she said. "It's wonderful. We'll buy it and you can use it for Gaithersburg and then mail it to us."

Now, Jack is Map Man. When we travel, I usually drive and his eyes are pinned to huge, detailed state atlases so that he can flawlessly guide our progress. I knew he wouldn't warm to Erica's idea but he did a pretty good job of hiding his reluctance. Off we went to Radio Shack where we bought a Garmin GPS device.

We carried our new purchase to the car, plugged it in and waited about five minutes for it to find the satellites. I was amazed. I can't even find my shoes in five minutes. Then we three generations eagerly listened to the liquid alto tones of the woman inside the machine.

"Proceed left on Delsea Drive for two point seven miles."

Okay. We did that.

"Turn right on Garden State Parkway in one hundred yards."

Whoosh! We passed the turn almost before she finished her little speech.

She took it well.

"Recalculating. Go one point seven miles; turn right on Shawcrest Road, then right on Wildwood Boulevard." She repeated this often, with mindless insistence.

Thing is, we knew where we were and we didn't want to go back to the parkway. I tried to explain this to her, but she was not a good listener.

Finally she caved and said, "Recalculating."

The poor darling spent a lot of time and energy recalculating but we finally reached our temporary home, agreeing that for the most part she had been right, and certainly well-meaning. But she didn't seem to grasp the big picture.

She had, however – because of Coastie Keith's skill – led us to a delightful restaurant for lunch, despite being disturbed that we were wandering so far off course. He had asked for Panini, and by golly she found it!

When we parted on day five, Erica and Randy flew to separate destinations (Randy had a meeting on the east coast). We returned Keith to the base where he was to do intensive training in hopes of gaining a spot for dive training, a highly competitive venture.

With Keith situated, we were ready for Gaithersburg. Jack set Ms Garmin on the dash in her little weighted case. He also had his *New Jersey DeLorme Atlas and Gazetteer* at the ready, open on his lap.

Ms G got right to it. "Turn right on Lafayette Street. Go two point seven miles to Garden State Parkway."

"We don't want the parkway," Jack said. "Turn left here." We were on Sandman Road. Jack said, "Go right on U.S. nine."

"Recalculating," said Ms Garmin.

After she seemed to understand what Jack was doing, things went along pretty well for a couple of miles.

Then, with some forcefulness she said, "Go one point nine miles and turn right on Delsea Drive."

"No, we want to stay on U.S. nine," said Jack.

"Recalculating." I swear there was a distinct edge in her voice.

For the next seven exits she tried valiantly to put us onto the parkway. We ignored her pleas to take exits on Edgewood, Indian Trail, Oyster Shell Bay and several more.

The Bible says no one can serve two masters. I felt conditioned to listen to Ms Garmin, but I wanted to maintain friendly relations with my husband. After some 20 miles I realized that this was not working. It was time for me to get religion.

I said to Ms Garmin, "Nothing personal, honey. We just think that you must be weary of recalculating. We're going to give you a little break."

I could almost hear a faint "Noooo. . ." as I unplugged her.

Gone and Forgotten

I passed the venerable Cadillac on the right at the place where west-bound Saginaw Street widens to three lanes. The Caddie hadn't aged gracefully. It had to be at least 30 years old.

When I was growing up in Michigan, sixty-plus years ago, I could identify every car, every model, every year. In those days it was all about Michigan. No one would have dreamed of trusting vehicles with names like Volkswagen, Honda or Mitsubishi. My lifelong habit  of identifying car model and year hasn't died completely, but the process has become so complex these days that I can't keep it going.

The paint on the Cadillac's pale blue trunk was so worn that a grayish undercoat showed through. A bicycle rack was bungee-strapped to the trunk; no bicycle. The car was rather low slung, even for 30 years ago. It had a sad aura of long-gone nobility.

As I passed I saw curb feelers on the driver's side, sticking out from the front and back fenders."Curb feelers! I remember curb feelers! Whatever happened to them?"

The darn things were hard to keep on. And it was still harder to make them stay in a position that would contact the curb when you backed, letting you know you were close, telling you it was time to snug the front end into position. We had them on our '55 Chevy Bel Air; on our '63 Mercury Meteor, on . . . I hadn't seen them in years. I remembered rusty, jettisoned (intentionally or not) feelers lying on streets and roads, in gutters.

Parallel parking was a big part of my driving lessons, many years ago. What trauma! My brother said, "Back until your outside rear fender lines up with the left headlight of the car behind you. Then straighten out and you'll be in good shape."

"What if there isn't a car behind me?" I wailed. "At the driver's test they just have these dinky little post things and you're supposed to pretend there's a curb there. I'll never make it."

"No, they find an actual, real place for you to back into," he said.

Even worse, I thought.

Years ago a friend told of a much, much older woman who went for her first driver's test. Probably she was nearing – gasp! – sixty. The man giving the test said, "Just back it up right here into this parking space, ma'am."

"Young man," she said in her most icy tone, "I don't back."

In those days you had to back. The sight of those curb feelers made me think about backing, parking, passing—things we really don't have to do very often today. Time was when stores lined a street and you had to wiggle into a space along the curb as close as possible to your destination. Not now. Parking lots abound. You can choose diagonal or straight in. No backing required.

Passing on a two lane road? Almost never necessary these days. Two lane roads are as quaint as Amish buggies. If you must travel for any distance on a busy two lane road, there are encouraging signs telling you there's a passing lane one or two miles ahead.

With the old Cadillac in my rear view mirror, I began to recall tire pumps in the trunk. Lap robes. Looped straps on the wall of the back seat. Evaporative coolers that hung outside a car window, dripping water. Fuzzy dice. Eight-track players. Bobble-head dolls. Statues of saints on the dash. Styrofoam balls on the antenna. Full size spare tires. Those things had all slipped away when I wasn't looking. Forgotten. Maybe not worth remembering.

But each one had its day. It's fun to recall them, to remember when discussions about the art of starting on an uphill grade could be downright lively.

No more curb feelers. Parking, cooling a car and starting on a hill no longer present any kind of challenge. We don't even kick tires any more. Our car windows open mostly to grab a parking pass. Kids can play video games and watch movies in the car, never having to bother with boring scenery.

It's called progress. And it is.

So why do I feel a sense of loss?

Homecoming

*I*n July of 1984 my husband's father, Bill, came to live with us. Bill's wife, Edith, had been placed in a nursing home near their home in Long Beach, California. My husband, Russ, and I lived 100 miles east in the high desert near Victorville.

After one night alone in the house, Bill called Russ. "I can't take it," he said. "Living alone in this house, I can't do it." So we welcomed him to our home.

During the next five months, Bill's condition steadily declined. One week, when it became clear he must get help, Russ made four 200-mile round trips with him to the hospital and/or doctor in Long Beach.

On the day before Christmas, after the fourth trip, the doctor sent Bill to a nearby care facility.

From the moment he arrived, Bill hated the nursing home. Early on Christmas morning, when we came to help get him settled, we found him sitting on a patio in the sun, holding a cup of coffee. How idyllic!

It was far from that. "Call the cops!" he said. "They've got some scam going on here, selling stolen cars." The soft music from a speaker above gave way to a commercial – for used cars. "Dad, that's a radio commercial," I said.

He was sad, miserable and confused. Everything was wrong. They locked him in at night, they watched him bathe, they yelled in the hall all night long. We located a manager who listened patiently to Bill's recital. We came to some terms: Bedsides down at night. Privacy in the shower. Grapefruit for breakfast. Maybe it would work. During the week, our daily visits produced nothing positive. This gentle, proud man was reduced to carping, raving, even to tears.

We fetched the priest. Religion had nothing to offer that Bill could accept.

Seven days later – on New Year's Eve – we were just back from another long day at the nursing home and had settled by the fireplace with a New Year's toast, when the phone rang.

"Don't answer it," I begged.

Russ said, "I'd better pick up. It's probably about Dad."

I heard Russ say, "Oh, hi, Grace." Grace lived next door to the folks in Long Beach. Russ listened for a few moments and said, "The lights are on? Can you tell who it is? Well, if you're not afraid, can you go over and check?"

Soon Grace called to report. "It's Dad," Russ said, hanging up. "He's in the house. She says he's okay. He didn't want her to tell us."

What to do? Russ called him immediately. A long discussion led to the conclusion that, since he insisted he was fine, getting along beautifully, he could stay there. We'd be down first thing in the morning.

We phoned the nursing home. They had no idea that he was gone, no idea what had happened, hadn't seen any strangers, hadn't noticed him wandering the halls. He must have gotten someone to spring him, drive him home. We were annoyed and bemused in equal parts – rather proud of him, in a way. Sly devil!

Early on New Year's morning we drove to Long Beach. In the living room we found Bill, sitting up, bed untouched, unable to get up.

"I can get up," he insisted.

"So, walk to the kitchen," Russ said.

He couldn't. For hours we pleaded, discussed, empathized. We brought in the McDonald's he requested; we agonized and wept. The lowest point occurred when Bill urinated in an empty milk carton while we were out of the room. He could not get up. He would not ask for help. We were at a complete loss.

After several hours we arrived at a compromise of sorts. He could stay home for a few days if his sister, Barbara, could come down from San Francisco to be with him while we looked for a different nursing home. We knew, of course, that another facility would make no difference whatsoever.

Saintly Barbara agreed to fly down, and I picked her up at the airport at around five in the afternoon. Later, troubled and worried, we left brother and sister and drove home.

The next day, January 2, was a work day for both of us. At around ten in the morning, Russ called me from his office. "Barb called. This morning Dad lay down to take a nap. He didn't wake up. He's gone," Russ said.

After a long moment I put the phone down as gently as possible. Bill, gone. He left us when he was in his own bed, in his own house, on his own terms.

He had simply wanted to go home.

Inconspicuous Consumption

I could have had four one-carat diamonds. Quality?

Whatever is whitest.

Maybe a sable jacket? No, I'd never want that.

New couch? Definitely.

Drapes? House cleaning service? Now, there's an idea.

But, no. We got a new roof.

It all began when I opened the door to a cubby-type opening in our bedroom to pull out my plastic bin of summer clothes. Slosh. The recessed top of the bin was full of water.

Water tends to work its way downward. But from where?

No water pipes anywhere near. Errant mountain stream in flat East Lansing? Nope. There had to be another reason.

It seems that seepage had been going on for months, if not years. Where old roof met newer roof, a joining that predated our ownership of the house, things had gone awry. Over time, the water had drained through the side wall, turning it into moist, rotting sawdust. The two roofs had never quite worked out the joining process.

If we must spend our savings, I'd like it to show. Who is ever going to say, "I love your new roof! It does wonders for the character of your house. It's darling!"? No one, that's who.

Replacement lumber in the side wall is now hidden behind our old aluminum siding. The new, white roof that repels heat in summer and captures it in winter is invisible except from across the side street on the corner of the next block. The short brick rooftop chimney, which needed extensive repair, now wears a pristine cover of shiny white lumber. It too will go largely unnoticed until it again becomes dysfunctional.

Sad. Just plain sad. But necessary. Like the two toilets we got a year or so ago. Taller, faster, wonderful, they refill in a fraction of the time the old ones did, and with less water. But no one has ever emerged from our guest bathroom saying, "What a great new toilet!" They would definitely say nice things if we got a new living room couch. They might not mean it, but they would say them anyway because a couch is obvious, visible and touchable – conspicuous consumption.

When our main house drain gave out ten years ago, we missed a wedding and ended up with a huge scar approximately the size of the Panama Canal across the back yard and down to the street in front. It was conspicuous, all right, but it did not enhance our situation in any way that we wanted to mention.

It seems almost unfair that keeping a house going has to take the place of adventurous vacations and décor that won't remind everyone of the avocado-and-Early American look that rocked us in the 1950s.

We consume, for sure. But we can't always consume what we want to consume.

Brussels sprouts, anyone?

Water Rover

*I*n 1962 our son Andy was four years old. He was a sturdy fellow who found four a perfect age for discovering his universe. This included his mom, dad and sister Erica, who was a year old.

In the kitchen on a fall morning Andy studied the back of the Cheerios box, which featured the Water Rover, a red plastic boat with a rubber band-powered paddle wheel at its stern. "Hours of bathtub fun!" said the blurb which included a picture of a boy holding the Rover, the requisite joyous expression on his four-year-old face.

Andy was intrigued. "I bet it goes a zillion miles an hour," he said. "I bet it goes this fast!" – swinging spoonfuls of cereal in a drippy, perilous arc.

"You can save your money, Andy, and we can fill out the order form and send for the Water Rover," I told him. Ever the teacher, I saw the teachable moment, a lesson in saving money.

Looking back over the years, I can't imagine how our four-year-old saved money. Surely he didn't get an allowance at so young an age. But I do recall that he gazed longingly at the Water Rover for a number of days before we gathered the requisite fifty cents, or whatever it was, to order the toy.

Painstakingly we cut out the order form and filled the lines, "Andy Armer, 2723 Butler Ave., Los Angeles 64, Calif." We taped the coins to the form and addressed the envelope, adding an extra stamp in case it was too heavy for only one. Excitement ran high.

On the opposite corner of Butler Avenue, several houses down, there was a mail box. We stood at the curb in front of our house determining when it would be perfectly safe for Andy to cross. Erica and I watched as he marched self-importantly toward the box. How small he looked, even at this slight distance, stocky legs marching, soft belly protruding ever so slightly.

He'd gone past a house or two when suddenly he stopped. "Mom! Mom!" he yelled.

"What? Are you okay?" I replied.

"Mom. Do Water Rovers hurt me?"

It occurred to me that he had no way of knowing how large the Water Rover really was. The boy on the box had held it toward the camera in the fashion of advertisers then and now.

Mothers don't often see their children at a distance. He'd looked small a moment before, but now he looked positively tiny, impossibly vulnerable.

"Oh, little boy," I thought." A Water Rover can't hurt you, but so many things in life can, and will. And I won't be watching from the other side of the street. I won't be able to help. And you don't yet know that this is true."

"No, Andy. Water Rovers won't hurt you, ever."

And he marched on toward the mail box, moving further and further away.

Faux Housekeeping

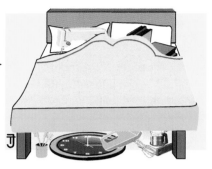

*C*omedienne Phyllis Diller said that she dabbed household bleach behind her ears just before her husband, Fang, came home in the evening. This was, of course, to prove that she had been scrubbing her heart out all day long.

But Phyllis was an amateur. All the bleach in the world can't hide disgusting messes. Enter Faux Housekeeping, an art learned by housekeepers over years of deception and deceit. After a number of traumatic experiences, usually involving unexpected drop-in company, cheating housekeepers learn how to appear organized while employing a repertoire of tricks that save time, energy and embarrassment.

Neatness is more easily observable than cleanliness. The best way to fake it is to tidy up regularly. Throw away old newspapers and clear table surfaces and chair seats. Dust is far more difficult to see than clutter. And remember: The floor is not a shelf.

Doing laundry is a lot like being pregnant. You are productive even while doing absolutely nothing. You can read a magazine while your laundry churns away in the washer or dryer. Are you wasting time? Certainly not – you are doing the laundry. Delay the transfer between washer and dryer and you can extend leisure activities for several hours. What's more, you can repeat this process for days on end.

Laundry is a never-ending task, a valuable asset for the born sloth. When company arrives you say, "Sorry about the mess, but I'm in the midst of doing laundry." Follow that remark by heading for the dryer and pulling out a load of clothes. You'll always find clothes in the dryer if you use this system.

In the bathroom, change the towels. Nothing speaks more eloquently of neglect than soggy, dingy towels. Put up fresh towels and you've instantly proved competency. Hide the disgusting bath mat and rug in the washing machine. Swish a hunk of damp toilet paper around in the sink. Throw cosmetics, comb and brush into a drawer or onto a shelf. Toss gooey soap shards and replace them with a new bar.

Empty the trash. Gather four or five tissues, clamp down on them with one foot and swoop that foot around the floor. It's amazing what adheres to this impromptu dust mop. Disgusting, of course, but the process is surprisingly effective.

The best indication of housekeeping competency in the kitchen is neat counter tops. Nobody's going to check the inside of the oven, but counter tops are impossible to conceal. Get rid of the clutter.

The dishwasher is an ideal place to hide dirty dishes. If the dishwasher is full, run it. Dirty dishes that won't fit into the dishwasher? In an emergency hide them in the oven. In the refrigerator, get rid of things that are obviously growing mold or turning exotic colors. Toss near-empty jars of mustard, salad dressings and the like. This will make room in the fridge for items that don't need refrigeration, but can hide there.

The kitchen floor is a challenge. The easiest way to live with it is to clean up spills and spots as they occur. If you can't readily see problem areas, run a dry mop around the floor. Dust from the mop will adhere to sticky spots. Wipe those spots with a damp paper towel.

Check outside the house for litter. Sweep the front porch. Wipe fingerprints off the front door. First impressions are lasting ones.

Faux housekeeping means that you don't have to drag buckets of soapy water, window cleaner, rags and vacuum cleaners from room to room. You are not proactive, you are reactive. Naturally, once in a while it's necessary to select one room and really clean it, even the places no one sees. But stop-gap measures work surprisingly well in giving the impression that you really know what you're doing, cleanliness-wise.

Fact is, you do know what you're doing. You are surviving, not obsessing. My mother used to call it "A lick and a promise." I've modified that to read, "A lick. No promises."

Two

*S*arah is two. She thinks two is very, very good. Everything is new – funny, exciting, wondrous, or, on occasion, frustrating.

She takes it all in stride, which isn't too difficult, partly because it's extremely difficult not to give in to a frustrated two-year-old.

What it must be like to see the world as entirely new!

Right now for her it's mostly pastel flowers, fluffy toys and finger food.

As soon as the frost begins to coat the pumpkin, so to speak, Sarah will realize that some actions have results and some events are not exclusively for her enjoyment. She will begin to see the why of things.

But at two she rarely has to worry about consequences. For the most part, there are none. Consequences appear later in life, and each negative outcome will leave its mark, a slightly darker spot in the perfect pastel of her life.

Two year olds have it made. Walking and running are relatively new, words are new, understanding comes in tiny, exciting segments.

Last Halloween, my husband, Grandpa Jack, and I were at Sarah's house. After trick-or-treating, Sarah and her four-year-old brother, Ethan, began to play with some new toys, slimy-looking flexible plastic lizards that parents (or grandparents) threw up to the ceiling where they stuck long enough to writhe and wriggle, finally dropping unwilling to the floor.

This was high excitement, as it turned out, because none of us could manage to catch the wily beasts. It was impossible to predict when their little gel-claws would let go.

This activity lasted for an ear-splitting amount of time. Sarah was determined to catch a lizard. But she soon realized that she was out-matched by all the taller types who shared her goal. She disappeared for a bit, returning with a small plastic step stool about a foot high.

She knew that she had solved her problem. She jumped onto the stool and realized that it wasn't up to the task. She didn't view this as tragedy (she saves tragedy for arguments over toys and such), and she tried relocating the stool several times.

Since no one ever caught a lizard, except when Daddy cheated and held her or Ethan up to within reach, she was entirely satisfied with her project.

We adults, objective as are all parents and grandparents, viewed Sarah's problem-solving effort as remarkable. If it was not entirely the stuff of genius, she outshone all that with her charm and unmatched two-year old optimism.

The Cracker Jar

I haven't seen it in fourteen years, not since I wrapped it carefully and stashed it in a heavy moving carton.

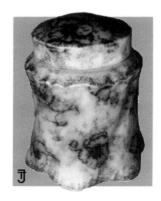

Last night I dreamed of it, a piece of china, maybe porcelain, maybe not. My grandfather gave it to my grandmother for a wedding anniversary.They lived on a farm in Minnesota where hard work was the unquestioned ethic, never spoken of, simply assumed.

It is a cracker jar, about twelve inches tall, shaped vaguely like a swirly tree trunk, flared at the bottom, the cover a cap with an inch-deep rim. The pattern is dark blue on a white background, a delicate tracing of flower-like shapes that seem to be shadows cast on the rippled surface-Delicate tracings of gold accent the jar's shoulders and the edges of the cover.

It has always been a favorite of mine because I have never seen another even remotely like it and I have always thought it lovely.

Part of its appeal is that it is enigmatic. Along about 1900 my grandfather, Martin Holmes, hitched up his team and drove the wagon to town, where his calloused farmer hands picked up this fragile bit of beauty. He bought it and took it home to place in the calloused hands of Emma Holmes. I see her wiping those hands on her apron and opening her gift. Did she think it a foolish expense? It seems too lovely to grace an oilcloth-covered table next to the woodstove. This jar should adorn a mahogany side-board in a spacious town house where it would enjoy frequent dustings from a uniformed maid

Did Martin's gift represent love or express emotions that he didn't feel comfortable voicing? Emma suffered severe diabetes and besides bearing two living daughters she had delivered two dead sons weighing twelve and fourteen pounds. They were too large to survive the birth process which nearly killed Emma, too. Without today's counseling resources and communication work-shops, how did Martin and Emma deal with such tragedies?

Martin died when I was only six years old and Emma when I was about twelve. I didn't know them intimately; we lived in Michigan and visited only once a year. Their life, to me, is mostly imagined. I see them working without letup on a farm that provided no room for luxuries.

And yet, there was the cracker jar. In 1996 I moved to Michigan from California. Not everything could make the move, so I packed the cracker jar and other treasures in a large carton, sending it to my daughter's home in Washington State. It lies there untouched, under the eaves. Before packing the box I photographed all its contents in groups. I glued the photos onto lined paper and wrote brief histories of each item, arrows pointing to their places in the photos. To read what I wrote is to read my family's stories.

The assortment of vases, serving bowls, cut glass and silver was part of the lives of great-grandparents, grandparents and my own life, including gifts from my children.

Will anyone in years to come know these stories? Will anyone be interested? They are my treasures. Is it fair to impose them on people who might not care and who certainly will not feel the emotional connection to them that I feel?

Maybe that is not what it is all about. Maybe these lovely things have already served their purpose. They have linked me to long-ago people, made them real for me. Over the years when these things were in my house they were a constant reminder of who I was and where I came from. To touch them was to touch my family members, no matter how long they had been gone.

Whatever role these things play in the future is not up to me. When the box is unpacked, I would like whoever opens it to enjoy looking at each item and then feel free to do with as they like without guilt. They won't be killing Mom or Grandma if they don't cherish them.

Mom and Grandma – Grandpa, too – will be just fine. We all had our chance to enjoy our treasures. That was our right, as it is the right of future generations to gather and enjoy theirs.

Romance

*I*t isn't over until the fat lady sings. It isn't over even then. Apparently it is never over. When you are nearly 73 years old, this is very good news.

Recently I have discovered that romance is forever a part of life, if you are lucky. Fat lady, thin lady, wrinkles, replacement parts, makes no difference.

Inevitably, sex got mixed up with the romance thing. From pre-teen days we were told that we needed to be really careful about you-know-what. It could lead to pregnancy and other things that we really and truly didn't want. We were also told that true love and romance transcend sexual love and make everything even more beautiful.

What we were not told is that this is as true at 80 as it is at 18. Shocked? I certainly was. When my father married for the second time at age 65 I knew he was ancient. "Quaint," I thought. "They won't be living alone."

After my 1996 wedding, I looked forward to quiet years watching my friends mellow and enjoy their gardens, their water aerobics and their library books. Instead, during the past few months I have witnessed the unbelievable. A 80-year-old widow said of her friend, "I really love him. He is a wonderful, wonderful man. But we're not going to marry, and we certainly aren't going to move in together. We both value our privacy. But this is the most joyous thing I could possibly have imagined."

Another friend who figured life as she knew it was over when her husband died years ago is suddenly twinkling, energetic, bubbly and joyous in a way that could mean only one thing – love, whatever form it is taking. "My remaining one-and-a-half hormones are raging," she reports, laughing.

There's more, but I will spare you. Friend number two, above, is a year or so younger than I am. Others tap-dancing around me are pushing 80 and even 90. My niece once said, "Older people never get touched. Did you ever think about that? Many of them are alone and no one hugs or even touches them. It is so sad."

She was right, as far as she knew. Certainly there are many older people who don't get touched. So some of them have lap dogs and docile cats, which we know is about the need to touch, to love.

We all have heard jokes about nursing homes, about clients tiptoeing around the halls, sneaking into each others' rooms. Perhaps it's about sex, but perhaps it's about being human, about touching, being touched, feeling affirmed as a person.

Romance is magic. It is wonderful.

At any age.

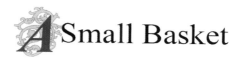A Small Basket

Beige and green grasses, woven tight,
It holds paper clips, pennies, small things.
I lift the lid, drop in a rubber band, and
for the first time in years, I really see it.

> I am a small child. We are "out west"
> where long-skirted women with small children
> herd sheep along dusty roadsides.
> At a trading post, Mom holds it.
> "Yes, it's nice," I say.

At first it kept my secrets; now, just things.
I pick it up, thinking of the woman who made it,
her long skirt, her children.
I press it to my cheek
My mother held this thing.
"Oh, Mom," I whisper.

First, Do No Harm

A few years ago I read Bruce Catton's magnificent words in his book, *Waiting for the Morning Train*. A delight at the beginning, the book later chronicled the ruination of Michigan's white pine forests and the decline of his native town, Benzonia, after the lumber supply was exhausted.

Once Catton established that the people of Benzonia lived in a kind of paradise, he went on to say that they were mostly unaware of what they were doing in the large scale – destroying the forests and ruining the environment.

"We were living in Indian summer and thought it was spring," he said. He likened that population to a ship whose pilot doesn't know – can't know – where it is going

What began as a tender reminiscence ended in mournful decrying of the foolishness of man who won't see what he is doing and can't know where his actions are leading.

Catton died in 1978, but nothing has improved since he wrote the book. My new *Audubon* magazine arrived, so for diversion I opened it, only to find pictures of dead songbirds laid out in shallow boxes by type – dozens of them, victims of cell phone towers.

On all sides I began to see signs of mankind's foolishness, wastefulness, inhumanity. Nothing seemed right.

I decided to share all this negativity with my husband, Jack. "This is one of those times," I said, "when it seems too depressing to open a newspaper because of all the insane, bad things we are doing to ourselves and the environment." I outlined the causes of my pessimism and he offered a few quotations and observations designed to restore perspective.

"First, do no harm," he quoted Hippocrates.

"Yeah, but, there's the rub," I said. "Define harm."

To some it's cell towers, to others Great Lakes drilling. Or, it's threatened Alaskan wilderness, even as we hear that we must have Alaskan oil in order to survive. On all sides there are controversies, each side telling us that they have solutions to our problems. How do we know who is right? How do we know which are genuine threats? How do we find the middle ground?

Is there middle ground? Radicals choose sides and feel they have the only answers. I feel helpless, and guilty, too, because I'm doing almost nothing regarding any of these issues.

Jack and I pondered a while, deciding eventually that the only harm we could define was harm we could clearly recognize. Maybe we could proceed by simply not adding to any identifiable harm in our own little spheres of influence. After all, as Catton pointed out, we don't really know what the future holds anyway.

Okay. That's how I would proceed: Do no harm that I could identify as harm. If everybody did that, maybe there would be hope for us.

Then help came from an unexpected direction. We tuned in to a book talk on CSPAN. An archeologist was talking about the bones of Kennewick Man, recently discovered on the banks of the Columbia River in Washington. Kennewick man turned out to be 9,600 years old. The author spoke about other ancient men and women found in the United States and Canada, few in number, but roughly from the same time period.

Kennewick man had a spear embedded in his hip, causing an injury which had apparently healed over. But according to the author it created an infection that would burst open occasionally. He would be in constant pain. Kennewick also had dents in his skull from old injuries, bad teeth and broken ribs that had never fused so that even the act of breathing would be painful. Other ancient men were similarly damaged. The author said that the average age at death was around 40. Women didn't seem to show the same severe damage, but their average age at death was 23.

The author spoke of these people almost with affection, seeing them as real people, faced with the problems of real people. He said that ten thousand years from now, humans would be unrecognizable to us in terms of race, lifestyle – any standard we use now to categorize ourselves.

Listening, I felt small, insignificant. But I also felt relieved. What we as a people do in the next year or two, or in one hundred years will not necessarily doom us – or for that matter, save us. Suddenly the problems of the present seemed less life-threatening. We can't control much. We really can't control anything, except possibly parts of our immediate little worlds.

If Kennewick Man and his contemporaries feared the future, certainly we who are in that future would fear their lives of constant threats, pain and illness. If our future meant going back to being Kennewick Man, we would be very, very afraid.

Bruce Catton says in his book, "Sooner or later you must move down an unknown road that leads beyond the range of the imagination, and the only certainty is that the trip has to be made. In this respect early youth is exactly like old age; it is a time of waiting before a big trip to an unknown destination. The chief difference is that youth waits for the morning limited and age waits for the night train."

It is what you do while waiting for the train that matters.

Three Weddings

*W*edding one: I was 22 years old. Groom, Bob, was 26, much older and wiser than I, it seemed. He was teaching in Los Angeles.

I, an East Lansing native, decided that Los Angeles looked very good.

Many months before the wedding, my mother asked, "What religion is Bob?"

"Oh, his family's Jewish, but he's not."

Mom kept a relatively straight face, a fact which I have appreciated more and more over the years.

Oh yes, the wedding: I walked down the aisle on my father's arm. The small Peoples Church chapel was stifling. June. Ninety-plus degrees, the occasional rain drop when the air was simply too heavy to contain it.

I was in some sort of ecstasy. The wedding ring about to be put on my finger would not be removed until my death. It was a crowning moment.

Blam! A flashbulb directly in my face. Fury overrode judgment. There was a rule against flashbulbs during ceremonies, but my wrath was all about the smashing of my once-in-a-lifetime dream.

I reached the altar to stand beside Bob. "Reverend Tefft! Reverend Tefft!" I whispered urgently. "Tell them to stop taking pictures!" The good reverend thought I was upset about broken rules. "It's all right," he assured me, and continued without a pause.

• *Marriage one, lesson one*: Some things just cannot be controlled.

Wedding two: I was 45 years old. Russ and I were to be married in Las Vegas, largely because my friend Jackie had insisted. "It has to be in our house," she said. "You must float down the staircase, a beautiful bride. It'll be perfect."

"Yeah, maybe," I said. But she was insistent. We rented hotel rooms for family, had everything in order.

But two weeks before the wedding, Jackie called. "Don (her husband) doesn't think the wedding will work, here. I'm sorry."

I wept. Russ and I searched out dingy rooms in fancy hotels. Nothing. Finally, friends Carl and Jo Lynn said, "Have it on our patio. The back yard is big. We'll put the tables there."

"What about the Steinway grand?" said Russ. He was determined to rent the instrument so that my son Andy could play during and after the wedding.

"It'll go on the patio," Carl assured us.

The date was May 13. "Guess you guys don't have triskadecaphobia," teased my daughter Erica.

The rental office was very skeptical about the Steinway on the patio, but finally they agreed. It never rains in Vegas, certainly not in May.

It rained. Oh, how it rained. It held off until after the ceremony, then dumped on the tables, the arrangements, the crepe paper – everything. In what seemed to be seconds the rental people arrived to rescue the Steinway. To whisk it away, in fact, improbable as that might sound.

"You can't!" yelled Russ. "It's fine under the patio roof! I already paid for it!"

They didn't even bother to respond. We dragged the tables inside and crammed them into Carl and Jo's tiny living room. Bare, beat-up tables and sodden folding chairs. It evoked homeless shelter, if not skid row.

But we were joyous. The cramming-in led to a whole lot of group jokes, stepping on one another and trying to squeeze past people without inappropriate touching. But there's something to be said for that, even.

• *Marriage two, lesson two*: Some things just cannot be controlled.

Wedding three: I was 64; Jack, 65. Our romance blossomed around the fact that email had been invented and Jack and I were about to share a high school class reunion, East Lansing High School, Class of 1949. On email, Jack looked very good. East Lansing had regained its luster after my many years in Los Angeles city, Phoenix, and northern Los Angeles County, arid and season-less places, all.

I traveled from California to visit Jack in East Lansing. Four days later we agreed that a wedding was on. At our ages, no time to waste. Almost the minute I got back to California, Jack phoned. "I thought we could get married in the old high school auditorium," he said.

"Sure, fine. Sounds good."

"I stopped on the way home from the airport," he said. "We can rent it for $100."

We had no formal invitations, just sent email to family, friends and co-workers and to all members of the class of '49. Quite a lot of them showed up.

At the rehearsal I told the minister that he didn't need to ask who would give me away. I was too old for that, surely.

At the wedding, he asked the question, "Who gives this woman?"

Oh no! I cringed. Then there was a shout from the audience, "We do! The Class of '49!" Jack had put them up to it, bless his heart.

• *Wedding three, lesson three*: Some things just cannot be controlled.

Sins of Omission

*S*mall objects, small lies. We might think that tiny things and little lies are unimportant, but it is those very things that can reach out to trap us – not every time, but when it happens, the result can be extraordinarily disagreeable.

Long ago, I was in seventh grade and new to East Lansing High School, a solid brick building that also housed the junior high.

Somewhere in that building I found a pen. Maybe it was lying on the terrazzo floors in the hall, or on the smelly cement floor of the gloomy locker room in the basement under the gym. Perhaps it was outside the building, near the bog that we crossed at the west end of Burcham Drive on our way to and from school. In any case, I picked it up.

The pen was definitely above average. It was a fountain pen, maybe a Schaeffer or a Parker, the kind that had a nifty little pull-out pump handle embedded in its side. You pried up the little handle, dipped the nib of the pen into the inkwell, and felt a small gurgle as you pushed the handle down. The pen was then suckling at the inkwell, a very satisfying experience, for us, if not for the pen.

I showed it to my mom. "That's a very expensive pen," she said. "Be sure to turn it in to the lost and found at school."

Days later she asked, "Did you turn in that pen?"

"Oh, yeah," I replied. In fact, it was still in my pocket, but a lie seemed easier than the truth. It wasn't that I coveted the pen, I simply forgot. And, I told myself, I was going to turn it in as soon as I remembered.

Weeks later I stood in the kitchen talking to Mom and unwrapping myself from the plaid winter coat that she had made. The pattern was a ghastly mix of tan, purple, black and gold, with a little bright red thrown in. It seemed to weigh nearly 50 pounds, and the fabric was incredibly itchy. But was it ever warm! Two minutes indoors and I was stripping it off as quickly as I could.

Which is what I was doing when I plunged my hand into the pocket and came out with the pen. Mom stared unbelievingly at it, her face a mix of horror and disappointment that is still etched in my memory.

I must have stammered something, but there really were no words. My body began to shut down. I probably had fibbed before, but never had I been exposed as a vile, bald-faced liar.

The next few days were nearly unbearable. I kept to my room for the most part, playing with toys I cared nothing about, nursing the pain in my gut while knowing that there was no cure.

Finally, on a Sunday afternoon, Mom came in and sat on my bed. Now, my mother rarely had an indecisive moment. I expected her to come down hard on me – no movies for a month, extra chores. When there was trouble, judgment was swift, after which sins were forgotten.

But this time she seemed different. We were to discuss the pen, that was clear. She had obviously given the matter a lot of thought and had come up with something so atypical of her, so indicative of the future of mothering that, had I realized what was happening, I would have been very concerned.

"I know you're having a difficult time giving up the pen," she said. "You want to keep it. I understand how you feel, but you have to return it, no matter how much you'd like to keep it. It's the only way."

I was dumbfounded. I never wanted to keep it. Whatever happened to consequences? How could I clear my name? I didn't think of it in that way then, but this new, empathetic mother was foreign to me. I wanted to tell her that I didn't have the pen any more, that I had returned it the day after our confrontation. But my 12 year-old logic said that if I told her that, I would be telling her that she had it all wrong, that she didn't really understand me. She was trying so hard that I couldn't do it.

But I had not received absolution. I had no way to make up for the sin I had committed. My mother, though she thought she understood, would forever think of me as a liar. I was left to live with all that guilt. There was no fix.

For months I wondered if she believed anything that I told her. I carefully edited my words so as to leave no wiggle room in any of my stories. But the conviction that I was a liar stayed with me.

A month or two later I was beginning to feel better about myself when Christmas arrived, bringing its excitement. Christmas was pure magic.

On the big day when she handed me a small package, Mother's facial expression was an odd mix of love and hope. I began to feel slightly ill. And there it was, a lovely Schaeffer pen, complete with little ink pump and trademark white dot, resting in its felt-lined box. It was beautiful. "Thanks, Mom. Thanks, Dad," I managed.

I don't think I ever used the pen. On that long-ago Christmas my parents expected me to experience a warm, fuzzy feeling. All I felt was acute embarrassment. But embedded in the embarrassment were two lessons that have served me well over the years. One was that those who love you, love unconditionally, no matter how evil you are.

And the second was that even if you didn't intend to be evil, that did not change a thing.

Decisions, Decisions

Making decisions seems to be getting increasingly difficult. I first noticed a growing problem during the infamous 1960s when lifestyles were – shall we say – fluid. The credos of some people were to express themselves by living life the way they thought it should be lived. If that proved to be too stressful they could assuage disappointments with booze, pot, or inventiveness in sexual matters.

In the '60s, "I'm not into it" arose as an okay phrase for getting out of almost anything that promised scant personal satisfaction.

I began to feel old during those years. We had young children. My husband and I were teachers, taxpayers – good citizens. We were raised with "do it or you'll be sorry" and "do it because I said so," and that was that.

In my parents' day the motivation was "we need to survive." Their parents, born around 1870, never thought of anything in life as being a matter of choice. They just did what they had to do. Perhaps too much introspection would have produced despair.

If I, as a young person, had told my mother that I wasn't "into" making my bed, she wouldn't have known what I was talking about. I can almost hear her saying, "What exactly has that got to do with anything?"

Mother was of strong stock. Born in 1898, she grew up on a farm where pleasure was never factored into the decision-making process. It was eat or starve, which meant plant, harvest, raise animals, slaughter – in short, grow and preserve almost all the family's food.

Choice? There was none.

Somewhere along the way we seem to have lost perspective. Some parents are in a bind, vacillating between "do it because I said so" and "do it because you might possibly be into it."

In the grocery store I have heard mothers ask two-year-olds what kind of juice they want. That's like asking an adult what kind of weaponry might be effective on the planet Jupiter.

Choices have multiplied exponentially, with no letup in sight. Five-year-old Jimmy has to choose between karate, soccer, beginning gymnastics, nature club, story time at the library or the latest video game for his age group. Mom asks him what he wants to do.

"I'm not into the story time," he finally ventures.

"Jimmy chose karate!" Mom says to Janet's mother.

Janet, also five, has picked beginning ballet, soccer, tumbling and story time. "Are you sure you really want to do all that?" her mother asks, thinking to herself, "Do *I* have time to do all that?" Janet is positive she can do it. She is also positive that she can fly an airplane, given a lesson or two.

It only gets worse as Jimmy and Janet get older. Sports, scouting, glee club, religious school, art enrichment and the like, all crammed into their childhoods, leading to college selection in what seems like a year or two after first grade.

I remember hearing, "You'll play the violin. There's one in the attic."

"You'll go to Michigan State and live at home. Maybe when you're a senior we can afford to have you stay in a dorm." Like a senior, even then, would be caught dead entering a dorm for the first time.

My father heard, "You'll have to take the horse and buggy to school. Too cold for you to walk three miles." And, "We're going to cut wild hay by the railroad tomorrow. It's selling for $3 a ton. Be up at four."

My grandparents probably heard, "When you've finished hoeing the back 30, come on in for dinner [lunch]. You can get the garden weeded this afternoon." And, "Take the bucket and get five gallons from the well to fill the stove. Then put the butter down the well in the bucket. Be sure you wrap it and don't let the bucket fill with so much water that you lose the butter."

I think of my parents when someone in our cosseted society struggles with decisions – "Do I want to?" "What if I change my mind?" "What if I don't like it?" The thought of even the slightest discomfort seems to paralyze – the fear that they might have to follow through even if whatever it is turns out to be distasteful.

Perhaps there is an up side to having many choices. Maybe we are happier when we are so much into something that we don't have to worry about boredom, grumpy co-workers, oppressive management and the other trials of the working life. But the reality is that almost any life process involves negative as well as positive experiences.

Here's a joke my mother often told: A young woman agonized, "Shall I get married, or shall I work?"

I understood it, but probably my grandchildren wouldn't. Life is work – marriage or career, it is all the same.

Nike says it pretty well. Just do it.

Awakening

When I was a child, Liberty Hyde Bailey Elementary School stood four-square, holding down the entire east side of the 300 block of Bailey Street in East Lansing, Michigan.

Constructed in 1922, the brick building had concrete floors and heavy double entry doors. Classroom windows reached almost from floor to ceiling. Back then, no one worried much about energy efficiency.

In 1937 our first grade classroom was one of two, a half-flight up on the second floor. Kindergarten was across the hall. On the kindergarten side were several small rooms, their doors always tightly closed. This was uncharted territory – we had no idea what lay within.

One fall day I was in trouble. I don't remember my infraction. I do remember that my crime was reported to our teacher, Miss Lillian Sontag, by Phyllis Schneckel, a plaid-dressed, pigtailed little wannabe teacher's pet whose desk paralleled mine. Phyllis was the first grade equivalent of the NKVD in Stalinist Russia, though we knew nothing of that at the time.

Probably I had been talking, or drawing on my spelling paper. Whatever it was, the teacher sentenced me to stand in the hall, a common punishment in days when teachers could actually let students out of their sight.

The hall's cold concrete floor echoed every footfall. I leaned against the beige plastered wall waiting for what was sure to come – Phyllis Schneckel emerging to gloat, jeer and discuss my transgression.

An opaque glass panel in the classroom door enabled one to make out bodies coming toward the door and the hazy shapes of movement within the room. I saw Phyllis raise her hand, doubtless asking to go to the bathroom. Doubtless not really needing to go.

As Phyllis approached the door I tiptoed across the hall as fast as I possibly could, trying not to make the slightest noise. I wasn't about to suffer the little fink if I could avoid it. I turned the handle of the nearest mystery door.

It opened!

Just as Phyllis emerged into the hall, I slipped inside. I heard her pause, shuffle about, call my name in a hoarse whisper, "Clarice! Where are you?" She waited. Then again, "Clarice?" A little less sure of herself this time. After a bit she went on toward the girl's bathroom. I could hear her steps, slow, searching, tentative.

The room I had entered contained a cot with pillow and folded blanket. The janitor's bedroom! Perfect logic for a six year-old mind. It never occurred to me that the janitor didn't live at the school. He was always there, firing up the boiler, swabbing floors or beating chalk from erasers outside the basement entry to his furnace room.

Of course Phyllis wasn't long in the bathroom.

Moments later I heard her steps click-clicking rapidly back to the room. The little snitch just couldn't wait to report me missing.

As soon as the door closed, I eased back to my station beside it. I could see Phyllis's blurred shape march to the teacher's desk and gesture eloquently, mouth probably in overdrive.

Miss Sontag opened the door and met my eyes. "Where were you?" she asked.

"Standing right here," said I with nary a flinch.

"Better come in, then." She seemed perplexed.

"Where were you?" hissed Phyllis as I took my seat across from her.

"Standing in the hall," I said, wide-eyed.

"Phyllis. No talking," said Miss Sontag.

A glorious sense of satisfaction swept over me, a growing feeling that marked both a beginning and an ending.

Years later I realized that it was the beginning of my self-determination. And I also knew that it was my first step toward the end of innocence.

Bonding

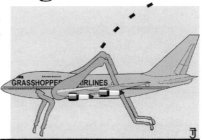

*I*n October of 2008, while on my way to Bend, Oregon to visit my children and their families, I sat in Detroit Metro Airport waiting for the plane to Portland.

After a two-hour wait, they said we could board – as soon as those in the Golden whatever, those needing extra, etc., or traveling with, etc., were all settled. I passed the first class people, all trying not to look entitled, and entered the main cabin – three seats on each side of an improbably narrow aisle. I plopped into my window seat, shoe-horned in for the long haul.

An excruciatingly slow procession struggled down the aisle, searching out seats, stowing luggage, climbing over one another with apologies. Finally most of them were seated, with the sort of determined resignation you see in hospital waiting rooms. Three of us were packed into our side of the aisle. Across from us, the seat on the aisle appeared to be the only empty one on the entire plane.

When the procession had slowed to a trickle, the man in the middle next to me suddenly leapt to his feet. He addressed a tall, dignified-looking black man who was folding his coat preparatory to settling into that empty aisle seat.

"Excuse me, sir?" my neighbor said, "would you consider trading with me? My daughter is next to you there and is terrified of flying."

The teenage girl gave him an eye-rolling, "Dad. Really!" look, but the newcomer allowed as how he could trade. The grateful dad thanked him, struggled out and plunked down next to his child with a satisfied sigh.

As my new partner settled, we exchanged a brief smile that said, "What can a person do?" He managed to convey that he would have preferred the aisle, but, hey . . . .

As we pushed westward I set my watch back three hours and alternated between trying to see the ground and concentrating on my book. My partner gave his undivided attention to a sports magazine. There was a little flurry when I carelessly moved my arm a fraction of an inch and my teensy plastic cup of ice spewed all over the three of us. Since the water in the cup was long gone, we were able to wiggle and shake most of the ice to the floor while we were neutralized in tray-down position.

After an hour or two I noticed that the woman on his other side had gotten up, so I said to my neighbor, "Maybe, since she's up, I can get out now for a bit." He crouched in a kind of mock stand while I tried to scoot past with a minimum of body contact.

But in his haste to make room he knocked his nearly full, uncapped, bottle of water onto her seat where it glugged enthusiastically. Horrified, he grabbed it. An attendant brought a few tiny napkins. We did our best with the puddle on the seat, but the damage was done,

When she returned he offered to trade, but she was stoic, assuring him she'd be fine. There were no other seats available, so she folded a couple of blankets donated by sympathetic passengers and settled herself, doubtless trying not to put all her weight down.

Much later the trademark, laconic voice of the pilot came over the intercom saying, "Well, folks, hope you enjoyed the flight. We're about to begin our approach to Portland. When we land, be sure you are in your seats with your seatbelts fastened. There are some pretty strong cross winds going on there. We should be on the ground in about 40 minutes."

There was a collective murmur of, "Oh – oh," but our craft remained stable. Nary a bump, not even through the lumbering dips and turns of landing. Not even when we heard the distinctive whine of wheels being lowered.

The ground rushed up at us and suddenly, "Wham!" The wind picked up the huge plane and slammed it down onto the runway, swatted it like a fly with such force that it made a gigantic bounce, fish-tailing to the side and back, then "Wham!" hitting it hard again causing another wild bounce before it careened mindlessly forward in what might have been the right direction.

Once we could tell that we were safely on the runway, everybody erupted with loud, nervous laughter, rapid-fire chatter, grins and high-fives all around.

Except for my neighbor and me. We looked down at our hands, joined together, locked in a rigid, bloodless grip. We laughed and said things like, "Look at that! We're holding hands! Man! Talk about scared!"

But we didn't let go, not right away. We were kind of frozen in place, maybe beginning to realize what had really happened here.

We'd had no time to think, no time to make any kind of decision. Whatever this was had come from eons ago when humans had to rely on one another just to stay alive. We had reached out to each other as people have done as long as man had been on earth.

When it was our turn to head up the aisle, we parted with brief goodbyes and a smile. I don't know about him, but I walked out into the terminal with a renewed sense of how very important we are to one another.

I understood that we need to take care of each other, simply because at the most basic level that's what humans do.

Rivalry

My daughter and I began our little competition on the phone. She was 2,500 miles away in Walla Walla, Washington, I in our East Lansing, Michigan kitchen. But we were close as ever.

"Guess what I did yesterday?" she said. "I took everything out of the pantry, scrubbed the shelves and put it all back in place. Perfect!"

Long ago I stopped playing the adult with her. She's 50. I am older than that. We're friends.

"Spices alphabetized?" I asked.

"Of course."

"Well, I took down the shower curtain, washed it and hung it back up."

"Really?" she said, quite smugly, "I scrubbed the cat box."

"The shower curtain was wrinkled when I hung it back up, so get this – I took it down and ironed it!"

"You actually found the iron?"

"Yeah, it was under that dusty pile of stuff to be mended in the linen closet."

"Good job. You would win, except that I straightened the junk drawer in the kitchen, and matched up all the loose socks in the sock drawer."

"You mean they weren't matched already? How long did that take, hours?"

"It went fast. I tossed about five with no mates."

"Probably the mates are under the bed," I said.

"No way! Yesterday I moved the bed and vacuumed under it."

"Whose kid are you, again? Oh, right. I win anyway. Because the ironed shower curtain still looked kinda sloppy. So I folded it into pleats and then tied the folds with strips of fabric. I left it like that overnight and, voila! Perfect pleats!"

"Well," she bragged, "I read that dryer sheets tend to clog the lint filter. You should scrub it regularly. I did that yesterday."

"Do you think we need a life?" I asked.

"Most likely," she replied. "I'm going to get a massage and have my nails done in a little bit."

I couldn't sit still for that one. "I'm getting a pedicure this afternoon, after I paint the living room."

She wasn't buying. "Oh! I have an interrupt call. It's the tour agent. We're going to the Hamptons, you know."

This woman going to the Hamptons would be like me shopping at . . . .

"There goes the doorbell!" I said, "I think it's UPS with my Tiffany order. Talk to you later."

We hung up. I smiled to myself, knowing that she was doing the exact same thing.

What Price Beauty?

*W*e can never be too rich or too thin. This philosophy seems to prevail in our society, but of the two, "never too thin" seems to be the clear winner, at least among women.

I recently tangled with an undergarment that I will call "Slimz" in order to avoid a possible lawsuit. The creator of this product is a billionaire, one of relatively few female billionaires in the world.

For the unenlightened, Slimz magically changes a woman's shape from sloppy to svelte. Actually, it's a torture device masquerading as underwear. It relentlessly shapes the body, punching in the gut, circling the fanny, and pushing up minimalistic boobs to the point of lasciviousness. Slimz renders the word "diet" nearly obsolete.

Several years ago, miserable about the fact that I had bulges where they shouldn't be, and, worse, that I had caused this with self-inflicted wounds such as those caused by brownies and lemon pie, I purchased a Slimz. Should be spelled $limz, believe you me.

When I brought my treasure home, I went up to the bedroom and shoved a dresser in front of the door, blocking it. Invariably, when you don't want someone to come in, that's exactly when they do. Feeling safe, I tried it on. Well, I tried to try it on. I started from the top, as one would to put on, say, a T-shirt. No go. It wrapped itself around my head. When it reached my shoulders it produced a force field that prevented movement in any direction. The top of the garment, having trapped my arms in a straight-up position, seemed to be trying to make my cheeks into breasts. By the time I managed to peel it off, I was sweating profusely. Several swatches of my hair went with it.

Unwilling to give up, I decided to step into it. In this instance the words "step into" involved wild hopping about and considerable thrashing on the bed, where I lay helpless as an overturned turtle tugging frantically in a semi-prone struggle.

Thirty exhausting minutes later I had actually managed to get the thing around my body – my oxygen-starved body, as it turned out. My face had a slightly bluish cast. I began to panic. Inch by painful inch I gained ground, tugging, rolling, attempting to shimmy my way to freedom.

Finally the garment lay like a punctured inner tube on the bedroom floor. I could swear it was panting. I certainly was.

Fast forward a week or so. I had borrowed a dress to wear to my grandson's wedding. It was a size small. I am not particularly big, but I am decidedly not small. The dress was lovely, but it spoke of my eating habits and my often lazy abs. Something had to be done.

In a department store lingerie section I spotted a garment that might do the trick. I tried it on. Not too bad, only minimal perspiration and maybe five minutes' manipulation. It would do nicely. The product was called "Non-fat Dressing."

At this writing, I haven't worn it to the wedding yet, that will be in a few weeks. However, I patiently await the day when Non-Fat Dressing passes Slimz in the billionaire department. Clearly there is desperate need for this sort of thing.

I'm thinking of developing my own product line. If I do, I'll probably become a trillionaire, because it will come with a hidden oxygen supply.

Snow Wars

Kids these days are bombarded with violence, in the media, video games, movies – everywhere. When I was a kid in the 1940s we had to make our own violence. And we did an excellent job, despite lack of help from outside sources.

There are two kinds of winter days, those when the snow will pack and those when it won't. On packing days, word sped around the neighborhood – time to build snow forts in the vacant lot.

Oh, boy!

After receiving battle orders we donned ten-pound woolen snow pants, interlined coats, knitted caps and mittens. Last came galoshes (probably a Slavic word for "snow in the socks"). Made of rubber with thin knit lining, they had metal hooks that poked through slotted buckles, then snapped shut. They were designed to slip over our shoes, but they never, ever slipped. Layers of clothing turned efforts to tug them on into major struggles. Galoshes somehow never quite met snow pants, so they acted as a kind of scoop to collect snow. All winter long, wet socks dripped from convenient protrusions in our houses.

The galosh struggle left us sweaty but battle-dressed. Plans usually included two snow forts facing off at a distance of some 30 feet. On our less combative days all of us (usually six to ten) worked together building both forts. Other days we chose sides, wooing the biggest, the most aggressive, the special buddy, trying to get allies who could produce a good, strong fortress for our side.

Building a snow fort is just like building a snow man, only on a larger scale. You start with a small snowball and roll it through fresh snow until it becomes so large and heavy that it won't roll any more. Be sure you are near your destination when this happens. You might need a teammate to help you hoist it onto the fort wall. One neighborhood kid discovered that on days when the snow was too cold to pack we could stuff it into bushel baskets and cartons, spray them lightly with a garden hose (de-iced) and let them freeze overnight. In the morning, after kicking, pounding and prying, we could liberate a fair assemblage of usable blocks.

Why make forts? Because they had obvious advantages. They were safe areas, places to duck into when you needed to dump your galoshes or shake your coat after someone stuffed snow down your neck.

But the fort was most valuable for storing ordinance. Once we all agreed that the walls were high enough, we began to gather ammunition. Most nearby snow had been used to make the forts, so we had to range rather far to get snowball material. We made our snowballs at the source, toted them to the fort, stacked them against a wall and set out again. Someone (the bossiest) had to remain at the armory to protect it. The guard always demanded more and more munitions. It was surprising how quickly they disappeared once the battle began.

During stockpiling someone eventually would decide, "Wait a minute. This isn't much fun."

They would know what to do – draw first blood. So . . . splat! The battle was on.

Rules of engagement changed minute to minute. We began with some shared understanding of what was okay and what was not, but as soon as it didn't fit our purposes we screamed out a new rule:

"You can't throw at me when I'm in the fort! You have to stay outside!"

"I am outside. My foot is outside. See?"

"No fair throwing at me when I'm picking up a snowball!"

"You weren't picking up a snowball, you were trying to sneak behind me!"

"I was putting on my mitten! You can't get me when my mitten is off!"

"I just got here! I didn't have time to get ready!"

"Leave my little sister alone!"

"Some little sister. She tried to trip me!"

"I'm in the safe zone!"

"The safe zone is way over there, by the window. What do you think a safe zone IS?"

"I was emptying out my galoshes. I wasn't playing!"

"If you're here, you're playing, stupid!"

"I said 'time out.' You cheated!"

"Did not."

"Did so!" (Repeat five or six times)

As you can see, today's kids just aren't as nice as we were.

.

Sometimes during the battle a frustrated combatant would head for R and R (home) sobbing and cursing, "You're all a bunch of big, fat dummies!" But he would return after a bit, armed with dry socks and a cookie, which he wouldn't share.

When we ran out of both ammunition and the will to make more, the battle ended. We all declared ourselves winners. We would flop on the snow, recalling choice moments in a kind of post-game play-by-play.

"You were so mad when I got you in the face. You should have seen yourself!"

"I wasn't mad, I just couldn't see. My glasses were all full of snow. Oh, gosh. Where are they, anyway?"

Cheating, rule changing and frozen extremities were tolerated in silence. We knew we would soon have the forts restocked and when they were, we didn't want to be excluded on grounds of over-sensitivity.

The worst insult was "bad sport." It was right up there with "sissy" or "crybaby." No other battle, such as summer water fights, rubber-band gun shootouts or games of cowboys and Indians, satisfied our killer instincts quite as well as did an epic snowball war.

Our parents didn't appear to be overly concerned about the occasional puffy lip or bloody nose. Violence among children wasn't much of a worry back then. They had other things on their minds, like the Depression, World War II and, a bit later, the atomic bomb.

We children didn't think of our snow wars as violence. Breaking rules, maybe, treachery and manipulation, certainly; but not violence.

If we analyzed the game at all, we would think of it as excitement sparked by delicious dashes of anarchy. Most of all, it was just plain fun.

The Large Family

*I*belong to an organi-
zation that meets in
June at an association
of cottages on a Michigan
lake. Our group uses the
middle cottages; others are
housed along the fringes.
Everyone shares the beach.

Each year the Large family occupies two or three fringe
cottages. We don't know their real names, so we use the word
"large" as both noun and adjective. Each year the term takes on
additional meaning. This family is large in numbers, large in size,
and most notably, large in love.

This year we observed a presumably-grandma Large and a
toddler Large analyze beach sand for almost two uninterrupted
hours. It was hard to tell who was educating whom, so intense
was their interaction. Time did not exist for either one.

Fathers were in charge of beach demeanor – proper storage of
canoes; float toys returned to the places where they were found.
A big attraction this year was the family's new, gigantic, inflat-
able raft, capable of supporting many Larges of all sizes.

When at the beach, playing baseball, or summoning young ones
for meals, fathers seemed to have no need to raise their voices.
The small Larges responded in turn – no arguing, no protest.

Afternoons, on a field in the center of the compound, an adult
Large or three played baseball – or some form of it – with an
assortment of kids. Small Larges giggled and laughed, staggered
crazily toward medium-sized Larges serving as bases.

One early evening there were only two Larges out, an almost-
six year old Large and a bigger, older Large who evidenced signs
of Down syndrome. We heard the younger Large yell encourage-
ment. "Way to go, Kenny! You almost got it! That was awesome!"
Kenny exhibited nothing but whole-bodied glee, bubbling with
excitement, loving every moment. When he connected with the
ball, he rolled on the grass, delighted with his success, until his
playmate called, "Now run over here, Kenny. I'm first base!"

At dinner time barbeques were fired up, and we could barely
resist the rich aromas of roasting chicken or ribs. From each cabin
family members emerged with side dishes of slaw, Jello, scalloped
potatoes and more. They met on a big deck central to their area.

Our group, observing this extended family, agreed that in our
next lives, we were definitely going to be small Larges.

Pilgrimage

*I*n 1941 my parents decided to take my brother and me on a trip through the far western United States. This was a big step for mid-westerners who had never ventured much beyond the states clustered around Lake Michigan. My nine-year old brain couldn't possibly appreciate what a giant step this was for them.

The prospect of war had begun to stir the country. Most parents weren't thinking about vacations. But with the trip in mind, the frugal Hoffers had dipped into savings to purchase a new 1941 Chevrolet. They must have reasoned that it could be many years before such a venture would again be possible. My brother Charles was almost twelve. Too soon he would be an adult. Better do it now.

They plotted carefully. We would see as many national parks as possible, explore the Pacific coast and work in a week with Mom's cousin Lee Bucheim in Orange, California.

Driving through Nebraska heat on two-lane highways, all windows wide open, we delighted in the fact that other drivers honked and waved, called out, "Hey! Michigan!" In Nebraska they didn't see Michigan licenses all that often.

We rented tourist cabins at four dollars a night, sometimes less. Generally clean, the flimsy cabins all seemed to have creaky floors, sagging beds and drippy sinks. Mom and I shared one double bed, Charles and Dad the other. Motels? Undreamed of.

Some gasoline pumps still had glass globes filled with golden gasoline that bubbled industriously during fill-ups. On average, gasoline was 19 cents a gallon that year.

At Bryce Canyon a switchback trail plunged downward. Charles and I jogged to the bottom, so narrow and deep that we could barely see the rim. A tiny stream meandered drunkenly, cooling sculpted arches and tunnels of every conceivable shade of rusty rose-pink. We struggled back up, panting. Charles shouted, "Mom! Dad! you gotta go down there! It's really something!"

We noticed a man pacing back and forth, very upset. "I left my camera case down there," he groaned, perspiring visibly even in the dry air. "Tell you what. You kids go get it, and I'll give you a dime."

We were off almost before the words were out of his mouth. Trudging back up the trail, we discussed what to do with our new-found wealth. At the top Mom took a Kodachrome shot of us holding the man's case, the exquisite formations of Bryce visible beyond our red faces and slumped shoulders.

In California we scoffed at tall palm trees sporting meager feather headdresses, so far up that we had to scrunch down in the car to see the top. "Man! Talk about ugly!" we chanted, again and again. Palm trees were supposed to be more or less at eye level, loaded with coconuts and with pretty girls under them.

In Orange, cousins Lee and Rilla Bucheim provided a week's respite from many days on the road. They took us swimming in the ocean at Huntington Beach and up into the San Bernardino mountains. They particularly wanted to show us a mountain lake. As the car skirted the edge of a little pond, they proudly said, "Isn't that just the prettiest lake?"

"You call that a LAKE?" I said, bewildered.

"Back home we'd call that a mud puddle!" added Charles. Mom switched on her full-blown dead-eye glare, so he added, "It's real nice, though. Bet you can catch lots of fish in there."

She had a few words for us when we got back to Orange that night. I didn't much care, I was busy admiring one of the highlights of my trip, the pull-chain toilet in the Bucheim bathroom.

Leaving Orange, we went to San Pedro, site of Los Angeles Harbor. Mom took a picture of an oil tanker anchored outside the breakwater. "That's the first Japanese ship to be refused American oil," she told us. We glanced up from our project, which was finding out if our popsicle sticks would have a message on them saying we could get another one for free.

Up on the hill above the harbor workmen were building many smallish concrete structures. "What'cha building?" we asked.

"Bathrooms for mermaids," they joked. When war broke out the following December my parents realized that those were gun installations.

We stopped to say hello to a distant relative in his dental office in Venice, California. He took us for a drive around the area. Along Ocean Boulevard, which ran adjacent to Ryan Aircraft in Santa Monica, he pointed out the camouflage netting above us, which stretched over the street for many blocks. "That's up there because of the war," he said.

War? Our parents had told us that this man struggled with a drinking problem, so we figured he was probably drunk. War? Nah.

Because we had a new car and were taking a six-week trip, some people along the way seemed to think that we were rich. But in our parents' view the trip was a necessary and valuable part of our education.

And we did learn. We learned through such sights as scaffolding still on the faces at Mt. Rushmore, one-lane gravel roads on the treacherous Bighorn Pass in Wyoming and the partially built Pitt River Bridge, hundreds of feet above us, that would be the road when Shasta Dam was completed.

We saw the wonders of Mesa Verdi, followed shortly by a night-long trip from Las Vegas to California. (You had to cross the Mojave Desert at night; this was long before air conditioning.) Everything was new to us – Old Faithful at Yellowstone, Glacier National Park, the California Redwoods, the Rocky Mountains, all forever fixed in our brains.

When you are a kid, you often don't know what gifts you are being given. But years later, when my brother and I refer to "our trip" we know exactly what we mean.

able

By the side of the road
a tiny fawn

the stillness of death

unlike any other.

A baby's white spots,

camouflage for the woods

useless here.

The Creator did his best

knowing nothing of cars

but everything

about my grief.

My Mothers Wedding Dress

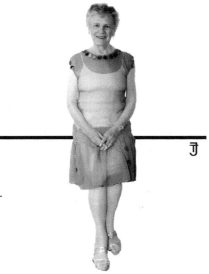

My mother, Luella Holmes Hoffer, was married on Thanksgiving Day, 1925. She and my dad, Russell Hoffer, met at the University of Minnesota when he was about to get his PhD and she her RN degree. The wedding dress was flapper-style, shaped much like a highly decorated pillowcase.

Mom was a farm girl, not a flapper, but for some reason she chose the latest thing for her wedding. I'm pretty sure it is the only such dress that she ever owned.

The wedding was held at her family's farm near tiny Morristown, Minnesota. Sadly, I never thought to ask about details such as how many were there, whether any of Dad's family came from Indiana, where he grew up, and countless other things.

In April, 2011, I gave a talk at a luncheon of the Michigan State University Community Club, the former Faculty Folk Club that my mother had joined in 1925. This is me wearing my mother's wedding dress for the event. The story is a transcript of that talk.

For the wedding Mom doubtless wore silk stockings, aided by a girdle whose job was to hold up the stockings. It's probable that in Mom's lifetime she didn't own much silk hosiery. In early days rayon hose were mostly used for dress-up. Around the house, I remember her wearing rather bulky full-length cotton hose, attached to a corset.

Mom's corsets weren't the "Gone with the Wind" kind with laces that poor Mammy yanked at with all her strength while Scarlett hugged a bed post. I remember her wearing a corset made of cotton, woven with elastic, with the extra insurance of embedded long, slim stays made of somewhat flexible steel, unlike the whalebone stays that had prevailed for at least a century. Her corset had garters which attached to the stockings. She had an ongoing supply of corsets – the ones that got saggy and lumpy with age were worn under a house dress.

Some of those house dresses were just one wearing away from the rag bag. When there was serious scrubbing to be done, the corset was attached to cotton hose full of snags and holes. These outfits were never, ever seen outside the house.

In the late '20s long pants were almost unheard of. What were then called "slacks" appeared only rarely until World War II, when it became clear that Rosie the Riveter's dress would snag on factory machines, at great risk to Rosie and the war effort.

Pants for women are one of the blessings that evolved from the war. Many advances, including the development of nylon, moved things along.

Sometime around the year 1926 my mother joined the Faculty Folk Club of then-named Michigan State College of Agriculture and Applied Science. My father, Russell Hoffer, a rural sociologist, was on the faculty. Faculty Folk meetings involved gloves, hats and hosiery that never saw a snag. The same outfit prevailed at most other women's organizations of the day. Members referred to one another as "Mrs. Emmons," or "Mrs. Mumford." On more formal occasions, "Mrs. Lloyd Emmons," and "Mrs. Eban Mumford." Nothing like "Louise," or "Pearl."

I don't recall a lot about Faculty Folk, since it was definitely off the radar of a little kid. I do remember that at a Faculty Folk bridge event my parents once won first prize – a chrome kitchen stool that was part of our household for many years.

Mom also was active in the East Lansing Child Study Club that focused on child development and eradicating unwanted behaviors, just like mom's groups today.

When she went to Peoples Church, Mom always wore a hat and gloves. Many women made their living as milliners in those days. Hat styles varied as much as did dress, shoe and other fashions. You could spend a dollar or a small fortune on a hat, depending on your check book and your place in society. Mom's hats were usually black or navy blue, always bought on sale. Her hats did *not* want to be noticed.

The Depression left its mark on the world of fashion, in the same way that World War II did. The only certain thing, it seems, is that whatever zany fashion trend comes along, it will be subject to what's going on in the world. What we wear speaks loudly of what we are.

To consider the procession from animal skins to togas to whale bone corsets and on to sweat shirts and blue jeans is to discover a great deal about the history of society's outlook on life, particularly its thoughts about women.

Mom died of an aneurism in 1958 at age 59. She never owned a pair of long pants, definitely never wore shorts or even split skirts. It seems to me quite possible that at this moment, she is hovering over me saying, "Now, let's not get too excited, Clarice – this is only a little wedding dress."

"But it's yours, Mom."

Hair

The Magical Thing Other People Can Do

*H*ere's a way to determine your age – your hair history. I have lived through:

✂<Electric permanent wave machines that belonged in the Marquis de Sade's rec room. Having a permanent involved risk of burned flesh and hair overcooked to the breaking point. As a child I waited for hours in linoleum-floored shops while my mother endured this torture. The odor was indescribable.

✂<Nightly pin curls. I didn't know for years that my hair was naturally curly.

✂<Home hair dryers, dome-shaped plastic with solid hoods. About 50 minutes' drying time was needed under one of these pastel-tinted 15-pound wonders.

✂<Home hair driers with shower-cap type hoods. Maybe a tad faster, but you were tethered long enough for the kids to eat all the cookies in the house.

Living through this history also involved:

✂<A haircut that left one inch of hair on my head. I had to buy a wig.

✂<A pony tail. During the growing process you could make two, a lower and a higher one for the illusion of a longer tail.

✂<Falls and rats. Shiny fake-fiber falls, which more or less matched your hair, made your pony tail long and luxuriant, like Debbie Reynolds's. Rats, disgusting hairy lumps worn under the hair, provided the incredible height needed for the fashionable bee-hive. If the fall or rat shifted or dropped, the entertainment value was extremely high.

✂<Hot rollers. These cooked for 20 to 30 minutes in a plastic bin before cooking your hair.

✂<Brush rollers. Not fun to sleep on.

✂<Sponge rollers. They had wire ends that bent back over embryonic curls. You could sleep on them. Sort of.

⊱Blow-drying and teasing. Teasing is combing your hair toward the scalp. Adding bulk, teasing produces a sort of home-grown rat.

⊱Home perms. Many home perms.

⊱Coloring - once. I didn't like it, so I put Clorox on my hair. Not good. Very bad.

⊱Salon perms. Many salon perms.

⊱Curling irons. These harked back to the days when they were heated on a wood stove. Now they plug in. This is called progress.

⊱Shock at people wearing frizzy. We all spent years, some even ironing their hair, to get rid of frizzy. What was this?

⊱Everyone wearing frizzy.

⊱Refusing to wear frizzy, marking myself as hopelessly old fashioned.

⊱Paying for all this nonsense as if I knew the secret number of a Swiss bank account.

⊱The latest: My hair dresser tugs my hair toward the top of my head, says, "See how that softens the jaw?" Like a soft jaw is going to somehow change my life. For the better, is the implication.

What I haven't lived through yet is coming to terms with my hair.

My sister-in-law's mother wouldn't cut her hair because when she became an angel she wanted long hair.

If angels have to deal with their hair, I am going somewhere else. Count on it.

Serendipity

On October 7, 2002 my grandson Keith and I waited at SeaTac Airport, in Seattle, Washington, for our flight to San Diego. We had come from Bend, Oregon, near Keith's home. This trip had been planned for several years, ever since I took Keith's older brother, Carl, to Seattle when he was about Keith's age. Keith would be 12 in two weeks.

At the gate we found seats next to a couple about my age. They were chatting and reading *USA Today*.

"We just left our grandchildren here in Seattle," the woman said. "I miss them already."

"We're bonding," I told her. "My sister takes her grandchildren on a trip when they're about Keith's age and she insisted I should do the same. She has fourteen grandchildren. I thought I could manage it with my three." I told her about the trip with Carl; what fun we'd had in Seattle.

"What a nice idea." She then told me a bit about her grandchildren.

"Where are you staying in San Diego?" she asked.

"Pacific Beach."

"That's where we live!" she exclaimed. I mentioned that our hotel was right on the beach and had a pool overlooking the ocean. We agreed that a pool was a must for an almost-12 year-old person. On the flight Keith and I busied ourselves taking snapshots of the Cascade Range, which he was seeing from above for the first time. Then we spotted La Pine, the little town seven miles from his home.

"Look at the blue roof! That's your school," I marveled. We took a picture, knowing that only we could know what it was—tiny shapes in the distance.

In San Diego we waved goodbye to the Pacific Beach couple and headed for a van that would take us to the car rental agency. Pacific Beach and the hotel offered everything Keith and I could possibly want. We toured San Diego attractions, but loved getting 'home' to the hotel where Keith dove non-stop for coins in the 84-degree pool.

On our second evening, a waterlogged Keith and I headed out for dinner, crossing the hotel lobby for the first time. Previously we had taken the elevator directly to the basement garage where our car was tucked away.

"Grandma, that looks like the lady from Seattle," Keith said, glimpsing someone walking out the hotel entrance.

"I think it is!" I said. "Hey! Lady from the plane!"

She stopped, turned and came toward us. "I made you some cookies," she said. "The people at the desk thought they could figure out which guests you were."

"Really? How wonderful of you. How did you ever find us?"

"Well, you'd mentioned the name of the hotel, and I was pretty sure they would be able to identify you."

I'd forgotten that I had told her the name of our hotel. We sat for a moment and chatted, exchanging names. "I'm Clarice Thompson, and this is Keith Gordon," I said.

"Thompson is our last name!" she exclaimed. They lived nearby, she said. I told her that I lived in Michigan. Keith said he was in sixth grade at La Pine Middle School. She hoped that we were having a good time.

"Oh, absolutely," I replied. "We've been to the zoo, Sea World and the harbor. And Keith has spent hours in the pool."

"If you need anything at all," she said, "Our phone number is on a note with the cookies."

"What a grand thing you did for us," I told her. "Sometimes when nice things like this happen, you begin to think the world will be okay after all."

"Isn't life wonderful?" she asked as we all headed out the door. We agreed. Life was wonderful indeed.

After dinner we picked up our cookies at the desk and read the note Jan Thompson had left with them. On the envelope she had written, "For the Grandmother and Grandson from Bend, Oregon. Hello! We met at the Seattle airport and I was so taken by your vacation plans. We wanted to especially welcome you to San Diego. An 'almost' 12 year old boy needs some home baked cookies! If we can lend a hand, call us at . . . . God Bless, Jan and Frank Thompson"

Her snickerdoodles were delicious, but not as delicious as our sense that all was right with the world. We knew we'd been given a gift that extended far beyond home baked cookies.

She'd given us a special memory and the knowledge that kindness could be found in the most unexpected places.

Games Children Play

When I was nearly four, I found Peter the teddy bear perched at the base of the tree on Christmas morning – love personified. He was the first stuffed animal that I remember receiving.

I preferred soft toys; they were more comfortable than dolls, more varied, more user-friendly. A few months later, on my birthday, Little Bear joined Peter. Little Bear was only about five inches tall with short-cropped yellow fur. He didn't seem to be terribly bright but I loved him nonetheless. Teeny, a polar bear who arrived next, was a little more stout than Peter and about the same height

Every Christmas a new stuffed animal greeted me, a practice that continued until I was far too old to tell anyone. Over the years each developed a definite personality. Brown Peter was bright and creative, Teeny conservative and thoughtful. Little Bear was pretty much a stooge. But Kitty ruled. When she marched in she immediately superseded all the others. She was obviously a female with her fluffy white fur, bright green eyes and prominent tail. To call her assertive would be an understatement.

My friends and I played with the animals, but the best and most secret play was with my brother who was far too masculine and, in his opinion, too old ever to admit to such girlish diversions. Charles and I created Basementville – in the basement, naturally. We hung blankets to divide the town, suspended bunk beds from furnace ducts, dragged doll furniture from upstairs and created a society.

At first Basementville was a lot like Utopia. Everyone got along. We made a clumsy boat to launch during our annual week at the lake. We made an airplane, painted red, that must have weighed 15 pounds, being largely composed of 2x4s, along with hundreds of nails. The *Basementville Times*, laboriously pecked out on an old Royal typewriter whose striking keys lay in a fan-shaped pattern, reported that the boat proved seaworthy with three bears aboard, which was the truth. In a later edition the *Times* reported that the airplane flew successfully, which was not the truth. The thing was so heavy we could hold it up for only a few minutes.

In 1941,when I was 9 and Charles almost 12, our world changed. The Japanese attacked Pearl Harbor and suddenly we were deluged with matters of war. We saved tin, fat and paper. We practiced black-outs, during which the air raid warden for our block would tell us whether any sliver of light leaked through our heavy drapes. At times I half expected enemy troops to come marching up our street, shooting everyone in sight.

Basementville was severely compromised by our anxieties about the future. Kitty began to gain power, then to abuse that power. She became a dictator, a despot. Everyone in Basementville had to bow to her will or be tossed into the laundry chute. My friend Carmen, privy to our secret games, dubbed her Mama Snowball, years before anyone heard of Papa Doc.

Soon the *Basementville Times* ceased publication. The blanket dividers disappeared. Eventually the bunk beds were gone. No one went near Basementville. Looking back on these events from an adult standpoint, I think the game had to end. We couldn't process the idea of suffering and lack of freedom in the outside world, and we certainly couldn't abide it in our own home.

Some 60 years later as I write this, I look up and see Peter, Teeny, Little Bear and Kitty perched on the dresser. They have rarely been out of my sight. When I moved from Los Angeles to Michigan in 1996 they sat just behind the driver's seat in my van, on top of my eclectic assortment of gear. They are a link to the child that I was, to the brother I love, and to my mother who clothed them when they lost their fur.

In other words, they are a part of me.

Recipe Secrets

*M*y recipe box is made of ugly dark green metal, scratched and dented. If I keep it on the kitchen counter, its rusty bottom leaves a stain. I've been meaning to replace it for about 45 years, get one of those nice oak ones; larger, maybe with stenciled designs. But I can't do that.

The recipe box is my autobiography. Sneakily, it's been chronicling my life. To go through it is to revisit loved ones, former neighbors, one-time work colleagues, dear departed relatives, friends of my parents – the list goes on and on.

Aunt Bess lived to age 95. When I was a bride she sent me dozens of handwritten recipes, practical ones, sounding just like her. "Aunt Bess' Chocolate Cake. Yum Yum!" "Aunt Bess' Baked Eggs. Good for last minute company." I don't think I ever made a single one of her recipes, but throwing them away is out of the question.

When I was newly married my mother contributed several recipes, usually on request. She used to make a delicious dessert that she called "dump cake." It had a broiled coconut and brown sugar topping. She sent the recipe: "Flour, sugar, eggs, soda, mix. 350 til done. Top with coconut, brown sugar, melted butter. Broil." I wrote her (this was long before the days of cheap long distance) and said, "Thanks for the recipe, but what do I do?" She wrote back telling me to grease the pan, preheat the oven, beat the eggs, add the dry ingredients in a certain order, etc. Then, hurting my feelings a bit, she said, "I didn't realize you knew so little about cooking."

Mrs. Howie lived across the street from us in the 1950s. She had a wonderful Scottish accent. When I see her recipe for scones baked on a griddle, I can hear her voice, "Careful, now, Dear. They can burn that quick."

Bucky's pecan puffs. Bucky was the secretary at Webster Junior High School in Los Angeles where my husband, Bob, taught. They did big cookie events at Webster in the 1950s and '60s.

One December day Bob came home at noon – unusual behavior – and said, "Tomorrow's the Christmas buffet thing. I need 15 dozen cookies."

"You're joking," I said.

"No. I really do. Right, John?" In a flash I realized why he'd brought fellow teacher John along – to prevent my strangling him.

Mary Matsuda's teriyaki marinade. Mary taught at Webster, too. Her teriyaki was the real thing.

The recipes I write are so cryptic that they make my mother's look positively wordy. I definitely know where I got it. Mine are mostly verbs, "Chop, mush together. Chill." I often find I need a couple of nouns to make them understandable. Flour and eggs come to mind.

I never seemed to bother with headings. I must have thought I'd know what things were from the ingredients. "Good mayo. 1/3 pickle relish 1/8 vinegar, lots of s & p." That's dressing – for potato salad, I think.

My recipes are on old pink "While You Were Out," message paper, on pieces of Christmas wrapping, on sticky notes saying "Amazon. com." They're hand written, in purple duplicator ink, mimeographed, xeroxed, and finally printed from e-mail – a whole history of modern communication in one rusty recipe box.

I have recipes for noodle pudding and brisket from Jewish neighbors; teriyaki from Japanese-American friends, salsa and rellenos from Hispanics. There are five or six "greatest baked beans ever" recipes; gelatin salads, seven-layer salads. Easy. Difficult. In between.

The oldest are Aunt Bess's. Then recipes from my mother and her friends; later co-workers, neighbors and my friends, finally those written in my daughter's handwriting – "Erica Ho-Wong's Chinese Chicken Salad." At least she used a heading.

Erica tells me her recipes are even more terse than mine. Some are 100 percent verbs, she says.

"Catch. Skin. Gut. Pound. Grate. Bake." Maybe that applies to poultry, maybe to possum. Who knows?

Some of my recipes are stained and greasy; others, almost un-touched, but in a loved one's handwriting. Some are seasonal, hauled out at holiday times. Some are dreams, fancy things cut from magazines – Duck l'Orange with liqueur, Finnish mushroom casserole – recipes that require the best china and silver. Probably I'll never use them but somehow the possibilities tease and they don't get tossed away.

My recipe box is a bit like a photo album. I can't just pull a recipe out and close the box. I hear voices of the past. Memories of long-ago dinner parties, pot lucks and family reunions hide in there, ready and waiting to tell me who I am and where I came from.

Stir, grate, chop?

Yes. Remember? Oh, yes, indeed.

The Raft

*I*n 1940, long before Polar Fleece and Goretex, spring days in East Lansing, Michigan involved wearing galoshes with nasty, pinching buckles. Kids wore knit wool caps that shed moisture up to a point, then took on water, doubling their weight. Snow pants were scratchy wool things, warm wet or dry, but heavy when wet.

Technically, spring had arrived, meaning that patches of ugly dirt had shed their covering of snow and were solid-looking but porous as pudding.

HUCKLEBERRY FINN : ON THE RAFT

The pond behind my friend's house had thawed, an irresistible magnet to us eight year-olds. Actually, the term "pond" wasn't very accurate. It was a greatly oversized mud puddle, a temporary hole maybe 4 to 6 feet deep, the size of two double garages. It was probably scooped out in the course of a winter-interrupted construction project. We didn't see ugliness, though. We saw a genuine pond, with fun waiting to happen.

Cooped up during much of the lengthy winter, we were ready for adventure. Near the pond were a few sodden timbers that we made into a Tom Sawyer raft. We'd be Tom and Huck, piloting the thing across the pond with a far-too-flexible willow stick.

There were six or seven of us, enough to play Indian Joe, Becky, various extras and even Aunt Polly if need be. We figured the raft would support all of us. Well, some of us figured it would.

It seemed prudent to test the thing before we all piled on. For some reason all eyes locked on me. I wasn't having it. "I'm not so sure it will hold us," I said. "Smith is little. Let her try it."

"No, no, Hoffer, It'll be fine. Just stand on it and see." Since we were Tom and Huck, we apparently had decided that using last names made us more like boys.

I regarded the mud-colored water. "No. I'm not doing it."

"We won't even push you out. Geez, what's the matter with you? Can't you even try? Honest, just stand on it. We won't push you out, really. We wouldn't do that!"

"Promise?"

"Promise. Scout's honor."

Scout's honor was sacred. At least as reliable as honest-to-God.

I was wearing my long yellow-orange and green plaid wool coat and the standard galoshes which came up maybe three inches over the ankle bone. Mist had been falling all day. The coat was getting heavier every minute. My mother had made it, and she didn't stint on the inner lining My snow pants were pretty dry, though, due to the length of the coat. If I didn't get any wetter I would be okay. I decided to give it a try.

Gingerly I placed one galosh, then a second on the soggy boards. The raft tilted ominously and I knew it was no go. As I turned to step off, I saw five or six eager faces grinning up at me, ten or twelve arms pushing mightily on the raft. With surprising speed it arced away from the muddy bank, separating itself from shore by what appeared to be six or eight feet. Too far to jump, for sure.

But jump I did, landing thigh deep in disgusting, icy brown water. My galoshes filled instantly, making my rush to the bank agonizingly slow.

Like a huge plaid lungfish emerging from primordial slime, I floundered toward shore, toward my so-called friends who were doubled over laughing, tears of glee running from their hateful, treacherous eyes.

At that moment I knew exactly what the term 'seeing red' meant. I saw red, literally. Murderously angry, I scrabbled at the muddy bank, trying to get out in time to clobber several of them into insensibility. With anger-blurred vision, I couldn't make them out clearly. They were just giggling blobs.

I clawed my way out, grabbed a two by four and started swinging. No longer laughing, they ran for their lives.

Lucky for me that they did. Sixty years later, I still remember the rage, remember seeing red. I know I would have tried to kill if I had connected with my weapon.

It was weeks before loneliness overcame me and I began to speak to them again.

But it was years and years before anyone of us mentioned the raft.

Woman vs Canyon

*I*n 2007, my friend Jean and her friend Dottie took on the Grand Canyon. The canyon won.

It went like this: They flew from Detroit to Phoenix, but not when they had planned. After hauling their luggage from the parking lot to the terminal they discovered that Dottie's purse was missing. They searched everywhere, returning to the car and checking along the route they had walked.

No identification for the Transportation Safety Authority, no boarding the plane.

The flight left without them. Dottie's son, who lives in the area, delivered money and a passport for his mother to prove her existence.

Eventually Jean and Dottie flew to Phoenix. The canyon trip was an Elderhostel. They were indeed elder, but not hostile. Lack of hostility is a virtue they both possessed, as you will see.

Elderhostel rates its trips according to difficulty.

"What was this trip rated?" I asked Jean after they returned home.

"Five."

"And what are the most difficult ones rated?"

"Six."

(Maybe that would be a little trek up Mt. Everest.)

On the first day, they were deposited by van at the bottom of the canyon, far from conventional tourist areas. There would be a five-mile hike along canyon walls.

Short hike like that? Nothing to it. However, as they trudged along, they couldn't help noticing that most of the miles involved a climb.

And almost immediately it became clear that the temperature was far above 90 degrees.

Lots of water needed. Jean had enough, but Dottie did not, and she became so dehydrated toward the end that the guides had to almost drag her to the van. They said, later, that they had serious doubts about her survival.

Jean was in trouble, too, but made it by moistening a bandana borrowed from a guide and plastering it onto the back of her neck.

After a night's rest, the group was again taken by van to the canyon floor where they followed a stream in blessed shade, stepping over rocks and learning about sedimentary matters.

Toward the end of the four-mile hike, Jean slipped on one of the rocks, landed on her face and got a black eye. She said that, for the remainder of the six-day trip, she looked "very, very menacing."

"People of faith would cross themselves at the sight of me," she said.

The following morning they walked down an 8-mile trail to the Supai Indian Village. Downhill made a difference, but they were pretty tired when they arrived.

For the rest of the trip they remained in the bottom, staying at the only motel for many miles, operated by the Supai. Their luggage came down by packhorse.

The week's educational adventures involved much about rock strata and native cultures, along with views of spectacular waterfalls. All very fine, since Dottie had recovered and Jean was mostly able to avoid eye contact.

Eventually it was time to leave, which meant time to go back up. Eight miles. There were three choices: walk (never), horseback (perhaps) and helicopter (only eight minutes and you can't see anything in eight minutes). Horses, it was.

Two miles along, still in the bottom of the canyon, Jean's horse – or plug – stumbled, launching her onto yet another rock. She hit high, no time to tuck and roll. Immediately she knew about the rib. Broken.

What she didn't learn until many days later was the collarbone. Also broken.

Soon after she came home, I looked at this agonized, hunched creature whose right shoulder was about eight inches lower than the left. "When you were hurt, what did you do?" I asked,

"Got back on the horse. No choice."

The plane trip back was okay. If she didn't breathe too deeply.

She and Dottie landed in Detroit along about midnight. Home at last!

Well, not exactly. No car keys, anywhere. They had them when they left. They began to search.

After pawing through their truly disgusting luggage to no avail, they rented a car, arriving at Dottie's house around 3:30 Sunday morning. Jean needed to lead her church choir in East Lansing, some 70 miles away. At nine a.m..

"Don't tell me," I said.

"Yep. I made it."

"You drove?"

She did. Black eye, broken collar bone, broken ribs and all.

"And you could conduct?"

"Kind of. Not too bad, actually."

"Would you do the trip again?"

"It was really great. But we did overestimate our abilities. Nothing over an Elderhostel-rated four from now on."

In the Mirror

*W*hat's this? Some kind of ancient map?

I'm standing in front of the bathroom mirror, ready to jump into the shower. I know better than to look in the mirror at this time. But some mischievous sprite forces me to glimpse my well-worn, unguarded body. I grapple frantically for denial. But, no. It's me, no doubt about it.

Last week at a writer's conference, our group leader asked us to write something – whatever came to mind. Just a few paragraphs, she said.

When four of us had finished she asked us to tell in one word the over-riding feeling or emotion of our piece. We said:

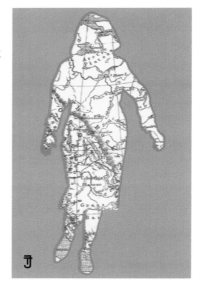

"Sad."

"Worried."

"Joyous."

"Frustrated."

"Now," she said, "try to find an opposite emotion in your piece and write about that."

Today, looking in the mirror, I see my body as a faded map of the United States, including Rocky Mountains and gulch-ridden Badlands. I remember that exercise and our assignment. I need an opposite emotion, and right now.

I think, "What if I am looking at a map of my life, here?" I search for evidence that my flaws and imperfections might tell me something, move me from criticism toward understanding and acceptance.

I notice a scarred knee down toward Oklahoma. That scar occurred around 1944 when I turned around, on my bike, to wave goodbye to Evaleen, and hit a rock and then the asphalt at about ten miles an hour.

Bicycle helmets weren't part of the culture then, any more than seat belts. Could have been my skull. But there's only the scar, which reminds me of Evaleen each time I notice it.

There are some fairly recent revisions, however. Near Ohio, I see a thin three-inch surgical scar. You'd almost have to know it was there in order to find it. Breast cancer, 2003. How can I not be grateful for that scar? It is a miracle.

Down toward Tennessee there's another, much more imposing surgical scar. It is at least five inches long, but it's almost as hard to see as the one in Ohio. On the last day of 2003, I received a new hip. Imagine! A new hip.

Talk about miracles! When I was a child I would occasionally see someone with an odd, stiff-legged gait, because one shoe was built up three or four inches. In 2003 my orthopedic surgeon told me that those people had their hip joints removed because there was no such thing as replacement back then.

In the mirror I see many little nicks and crevasses that have blended in over the years, leaving only surface clues of possible archeological sites.

Far north of it all is my face, but I see it so frequently that it no longer has the power to shock me. Same with my hands. Nothing much to do about hands, as many an aging actress would testify. I look into my eyes, and what I see there, this minute, is sudden understanding and a big dose of wry amusement. What exactly is so important, here, gulches and bumps or the fact that I am one very lucky person? The eyes tell me to get over it.

I have found the opposite emotion. Dissatisfaction has been replaced – with pure, joyous, gratitude.

Special Moments

Parenting is a tough job, certainly, but not without its rewards. Looking back (really back – these critters arrived in 1958 and 1961) I seem to remember negative experiences more than positive ones. Why? Because the negatives are a lot funnier. The horrible stab of guilt that cripples one at the moment of collapse turns out to provide the most humor once the patina of time has done its work and you realize that somehow the kid survived.

I offer a few stories for our younger readers, just in case they think they might have forever ruined their children's lives.

My daughter, Erica was about four years old when her grandmother bought her a red sailor dress. It was the epitome of cute, pleated skirt attached to a yoke, navy blue sailor collar with white braid and a snappy navy blue tie. Alas, it was 100% cotton.

Permanent press had been invented around the time Erica was born and I had forgotten a lot about ironing. Let's just say ironing wasn't my passion. (As a bride I went to Sears to buy an ironing board cover. One of these boasted, "Guaranteed for 15 Years!" The thought of ironing for the next fifteen years sent me clean out of the store.)

Erica wore the dress with pride once or twice. Then it was laundered and put into the ironing basket. She asked about it from time to time, receiving weak assurances that it would be ready soon. Eventually I got around to the chore and did an acceptable job on the subject garment. Proudly, I hung it in her closet. A day or so later she came into the kitchen, hot tears rolling down her cheeks.

"Look!" she sobbed."You never iron. Look at my dress!"

The dress cleared her waist nicely, stopping at midpoint on her hips. Large stab of guilt. Huge. I guessed it had been ten months, maybe a year since I had applied myself to the ironing basket.

"I'm so sorry, honey," I tried to hug her as she shied away. "Maybe we can buy some navy pants and you can wear it as a top." Erica wasn't having any. I had been found out, big time.

I belonged to a neighborhood bridge group, four mommies who gathered once a week at someone's home for cards, gossip and dessert – not necessarily in that order. It was my turn to host the group and a pie was cooling on the kitchen table when Erica, about 6, entered.

She scoped out the situation and said in the most pathetic *Les Miserables* voice you could imagine, "Mommy, if there's any pie left after the bridge group can I have some?"

For a moment I was stunned. Was it true that the only desserts I made were for others, never the family? Darn tootin'. When it came to dessert my family was plain out of luck. My husband didn't care for dessert, I didn't need it, and since the cookie jar was reloaded almost daily this dessert dearth hadn't occurred to me, let alone been a cause for worry.

"Of course you can have some," I said, "First thing in the morning. For breakfast, if you want." How she had managed to look like a starveling was amazing. Poor little thing, probably hardly knew what pie tasted like. Another stab. More pangs of guilt.

Most likely an issue of *Parents Magazine* came out around that time with articles about making Wizard of Oz cupcakes or Jell-O in the shape of a watermelon. These do nothing to increase a mother's parenting confidence. You gain the impression that all but the laziest, most uncaring mothers in the world would ignore a child's simple pleasure in such niceties. (These pieces invariably say things like "Ten minutes to quick treats," leaving the cook with ten dirty pots and pans, a floor to mop and several hours gone. Not only that, the Wizard of Oz cupcakes look more like Picasso in profile than Cowardly Lion.)

My finest mothering moment, one that I almost hate to admit, occurred when my son Andy was about three. At around 2 a.m. I heard him calling me. Just as I hit the door he threw up mightily all over himself and his bed. I bathed him, gathered the soiled linens and re-made the bed. Feeling better, wearing clean pajamas he sank onto the fresh sheets, gave me a beatific smile and said, "It's good to throw up 'cause you get to have a clean bed."

Astonishment was followed by a quick assessment: Did I really change his bed that infrequently? Surely not. These many years later I still have to tell myself occasionally that what Andy really meant was that the clean bed smelled and felt so good after his awful experience.

I carried that one around with me for quite a while. Guess who saved me? Erma Bombeck. Dear Erma, my idol and role model. She said it in black and white, *in italics even* – her awful mothering moment. Seems she was in the grocery store with her young son who was riding in the cart. The aisle was quite crowded so she reached rather far to grab something from a high shelf. As she put it, "He flinched!" Only one way to interpret that: bad, child-beating mother.

We need to bear in mind that perfection is a goal, not a reality. Kids are pretty resilient. They can survive us, perhaps even better than we can survive them. It's laughter that provides leavening in the relationship. Never despair. Just think, there might be another devastating experience just around the corner.

Breaking Away

*I*n 1954 my parents planned to drive from Michigan to Nashville, Tennessee, during spring break. I was there working on a master's degree at George Peabody College for Teachers, but mostly I was deciding whether to marry Bob, a flute teacher from Los Angeles.

We had met two summers before at Interlochen Music Camp in northern Michigan. He was on leave, going to Peabody for a master's degree. By the next year he decided to get a second master's – if I would join him and get a master's.

"We could get better acquainted," he said. Sounded good to me.

I was lucky to get a job as last chair viola in the Nashville Symphony and I applied for and received a scholarship. I was on my way.

That spring we looked forward to showing my parents the Parthenon, The Hermitage (Andrew Jackson's estate) and other Nashville attractions. We were far too snobby to take them to the Ryman Auditorium, home of The Grand Ole Opry. We were classical musicians, after all.

On Valentine's Day Bob and I became officially engaged and we began to plan a June wedding. When we called my parents with our joyous news, Mother immediately said, "You can wear Marjorie's wedding dress."

She had made the dress the previous fall for my brother's bride. My mother was an excellent seamstress. All my life she had made my clothes, and because of this my idea of excitement was to wear something "store-bought." I was not enthusiastic about wearing the dress my brother's wife had worn. I wanted my own dress.

Without thinking, I said, "I really want to buy my wedding dress." We hung up with much less joy and without a resolution.

A few days later I got a letter from Mom. It said, "Since you are buying a wedding dress, we won't be able to come down to Nashville during spring break. It's just too expensive."

I was shocked and bewildered. This was so unlike my mother. I had never known her to be manipulative (I didn't really know the term then).

But I did know that the issue wasn't money, wasn't even buying the dress. It was her feelings, and it hurt me that I was the one who had caused her pain.

I had lived at home all my life, including four years at Michigan State College. My mother had always been in charge and I had never really dealt with being a separate, adult person. I knew that I stood at a crossroads.

I sought out Lyle, another graduate student, thinking he would know what to do. He was old, probably at least 32. He was married. I needed to talk to someone who knew about these kinds of things. We sat in the sun on the front steps of my graduate women's dorm and talked for a long time. This was more than 50 years ago and I don't remember exactly what was said, but I know wise old Lyle helped me. He was clearly ready for his career in counseling. Somehow he made me understand the situation and helped me fashion a few tools that I could use to deal with it – tools I have used many times since.

A few days later I answered my mother's letter, saying, in essence, "I'm really sorry you won't be able to visit during spring break. We were looking forward to it. And I am very sorry that I hurt your feelings. It wasn't intentional, believe me. You are the best mom possible, and I love you."

My folks came to Nashville. We had a fine time seeing the places Bob and I had selected. At the store, I modeled my dress for my mother. It cost $97, modest even for those times.

She approved.

Road Trips!

hen I was a child, summer meant traveling to Minnesota to visit my grandparents on the farm near Morristown, a tiny town south of Minneapolis.

From my earliest memory to age seven, the trip was in our 1936 Oldsmobile, a dark green 4-door model with an exterior running board step. My brother Charles and I hunkered down in the back seat, giggling, gossiping and commenting on the passing scene. We were never bored – there was always something to see.

Since the trip was more than 600 miles on two-lane highways and included creeping through the Chicago area, it involved an overnight stop.

Leaving East Lansing, we headed south. I knew we were really and truly on our way when we reached US 12, the major Detroit-Chicago artery, near Jackson. A few hours later, Gary, Indiana gave views of a world that I could barely comprehend – tiny dark houses with almost no yards, crammed together under more power lines than I thought possible. Huge smokestacks loomed in the background near Lake Michigan. Gary was a steel town then, and evidence of that was everywhere, so much so that even a six year-old could see that the grit, smoke and crowding comprised a dusky world far removed from East Lansing, Michigan.

Through northern Illinois, rolling green hills provided an Eden for thousands of Holstein dairy cattle, who during summer months knew the inside of a barn only at milking time.

We stopped at service stations where the attendant filled the tank from gasoline pumps supporting glass tanks. I could see large air bubbles rising as the fuel went out. Dad supervised while the attendant checked the tire pressure and grabbed a rag to cautiously open the radiator and check the water level. Too often, people were scalded opening boiling, steaming radiators. After that, our man checked the oil, cleaned the windshield and we were on our way.

Lunch was along the highway. Signs announced "Roadside Table," and that's what they were – a table and trash can in a small clearing. We had sandwiches from home wrapped in waxed paper, homegrown tomatoes sliced on site and seasonal Michigan fruit, which had no peer.

The overnight stop was in some small town where a "Rooms for Tourists" sign could be found. Enterprising residents could rent a room or two and pick up a few extra dollars. The norm was a shared bathroom – shared with everyone in the house – and two double beds, made up with old quilts and brick-like pillows. No one thought of breakfast, these were Bed and Nothing Else.

As we drove along, Charles and I stuck our hands out the windows to feel the rushing air, which at 50 miles an hour provided resistance enough to float our hands, shaped into stiff wings.

Because car windows were seldom closed in summer, an errant bee would occasionally blow in, causing considerable excitement for passengers and driver. It was hard for Dad to concentrate on the road with everyone flailing about, swatting, shouting, trying to get the bee, whose only wish was to be free of this madness.

"There he is!"

"Where?"

"On Dad's shoulder! No, wait. On his head!"

At such times the car would swerve dramatically.

When we reached Minnesota, our Michigan license plates were an object of interest to the natives. In those years the plates were on both front and back. Along the two-lane highway beside the Mississippi River, oncoming cars would honk and the people would wave.

Sometimes a driver would call out, "Hey, Michigan!"

We felt very special indeed.

Author David McCullough once said, "Nobody ever lived in the past. [They] never walked around saying how great it was living in the past." Our little family thought the past was oxen pulling covered wagons. We zipped along concrete highways in a car that was pure luxury. We knew that we were the luckiest people on earth. And in many ways, we were.

To Catch a Cat

*T*oday is the day to take our cat to the vet. Husband Jack and I double check the calendar. Sure enough, no way to get out of it.

Thoughts of mobile vets come to mind. They would bring a van to the house, but we'd still have to catch the cat. A few times in the past we've had to cancel at the last minute because we were unable to corral her and stuff her into the carrier.

This is an extremely speedy and skittish cat. She has a multi-gigabyte memory and the intuition of the Dalai Lama. She can read volumes in the smallest gesture, the slightest sound. Running past us, she breaks the kitty sound barrier. We don't realize she's been there until she's gone.

But she is the most affectionate cat we have ever known. She streaks ahead as we are going upstairs, then plops down on a high step to await petting. When I make the bed, we have to play "find the kitty" which involves tickling and roughing up the zigzagging cat lump under the covers.

We begin to strategize our approach long before time to leave. General Eisenhower in Europe during World War II could not have planned his invasion more carefully than we plan ours.

I whisper to Jack, "Do you know where the C-A-R-R-I-E-R is?"

"It's in the G-U-E-S-T room."

"Uh-oh, she is sleeping in there right now."

"Rattle the food dish. Maybe she'll come out."

"Did you close all the bedroom and bathroom doors?"

"Yes, and the basement door, but I had to close it kind of hard, so she might have heard it."

In slow motion I open the hall closet door to silently remove my jacket. I disturb not a molecule of air. I don't put the jacket on. Doing that would give it away and sink the whole operation. She doesn't need to actually see me put it on, she will just know. I tuck it out of sight under the couch pillows.

We need to leave in about ten minutes. Entering the guest room where she sleeps, Jack rattles some pages in his book and whistles with forced nonchalance as he closes in.

I dare not enter the room. Two on one would be a dead giveaway. Someone would be maimed, if not killed. And it wouldn't necessarily be the cat.

I ease shut one of the two doors leading into the room. The other door opens to a bathroom that adjoins the kitchen. She can get to the bathroom, but no farther, since the exit to the kitchen is closed. As far as we are aware, she can't crawl down the tub drain, and naturally we have shut the toilet lid.

Listening at the door, I hear no yowls, hisses, or other indications of trouble. Still, I begin to worry. What if she's hiding in the inch of space under the dresser? What if he has to sprain her tail, grabbing her? But before long Jack emerges bearing carrier and enraged cat.

"Nothing to it," he says. (He's a guy, of course.) I check him for claw marks. None that show. Good.

In the car we explain to our furious passenger that we are doing this for her own good. We know this is a meaningless exercise, but it makes us feel better.

She can't hear us anyway. She is too busy inventing new cat curses. Perhaps she'll forgive us in time for dinner.

The Ugly Tree

*I*n the early 1980s my husband, Russ, and I lived in a small concrete block house that clung to the east side of the west-rising San Bernardino Mountains in California's Mojave Desert. We had bought the house on impulse during a Sunday drive. Smitten by the endless view of Apple Valley and Hesperia snuggled far below, we were goners from the

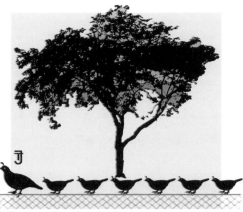

minute we spotted the "For Sale" sign clinging to the steep, rocky edge of Roundup Way, our road.

An old locust tree dominated a large percentage of our tiny shelf of front yard. Soon we discovered that the tree not only blocked part of our vista, its roots sent up hundreds of tiny shoots – some sort of tree plan for immortality, apparently.

"That tree has got to go," I said on more than one occasion. It was ugly, its crown a tangle of no discernable design.

Russ agreed. "It looks like something you'd pull out of a hairbrush."

One early summer evening, lounging on the front stoop, we heard a subtle muttering, clucking kind of sound. Our two dogs sat up, pricked their ears and gazed to the right. A small bird, a California Quail, rounded the corner of the house, his one-feather crest bobbing over his beak.

Almost nothing is more entrancing than a pedestrian quail. We knew this one was a male because female quail don't sport that jaunty head-dress. He burbled a gentle summons and soon a few families joined him, followed by many, many more.

Apparently he was only a forward scout; quail are seldom alone. The dogs didn't seem to feel the need to protect us from these critters. They were as interested in this mass exodus as we were.

Beneath the locust tree a chain link fence fronted Roundup Way. Our visitors mounted it, lining up along the top for a good 25 feet. They preened, fluffed and muttered, apparently taking a little break. One couldn't help wondering what terrible situation they had left behind. What had caused them to embark on a trek that might extend far beyond our road, maybe far beyond Apple Valley?

As the evening darkened, our visitors continued to discuss various aspects of their situation. Suddenly, without the slightest outward sign, they rose in a single cloud and disappeared into the locust tree. Then we heard scuffling, peeping, scratching, wiggling and lots of dialog as they began to sort out who would go where, which was the best location. It was almost as if the babies were calling, "I'm thirsty! Sarah is crowding me! I don't want to be next to Henry!"

The parents spoke in clearly understandable Quail, "It's quiet time now. Be very still." "No, the coyotes are way up the mountain, sound asleep." There was even the occasional, "Don't make me come up there!"

This scenario became a regular feature of our summer twilight hours. As the birds marched past us each evening we began to recognize individuals – old Limpy, hyperactive young Harold, gossipy Gertrude. The lead quail we named "George," for General Patton, of course. The ugliness of the tree began to recede as our fondness for its occupants increased. No way could we summon some behemoth piece of equipment to level our friends' home. For what? A green lawn that we would have to water constantly, feed and nurture through impossible desert conditions?

"Something there is," wrote poet Robert Frost, "that doesn't love a wall."

Something there is, Russ and I decided, that loves a small quail, that helps us to realize what truly nourishes the human soul.

And that would include the locust tree.

Medical Matters :
The Olden Days

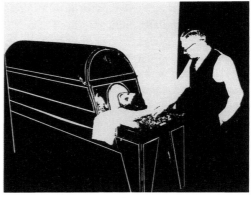

*M*y father often said that an advantage of aging is watching how things turn out.

How right he was!

Perhaps the most interesting phenomenon I have experienced during my 70-plus years is the evolution of medical treatment. Some of my memories are so markedly different from the way things are done today that they seem almost medieval.

When I was young it was not uncommon to see double leg amputees scooting about on low wooden platforms with casters. The rider pushed himself along with short leather-covered posts held in gloved hands. He needed a hard surface, so he had to stay on the sidewalk. Stairs were out of the question.

In the 1930s wheel chairs were rarely seen. Handicap accessibility was unheard of. Doors were narrow, ramps nonexistent. If you were confined to a wheel chair, you pretty much stayed home.

Today we have vans with lifts and lightweight wheel chairs that fold to fit into car trunks.

An orthopedic surgeon recently said to me, "Remember when you were a kid, you would see people with one shoe built up on a thick platform?"

I certainly did remember.

He went on to say that many of these were people whose hips were so damaged by arthritis that the joint was removed and the bones fused, causing a loss of four or so inches to the leg.

When I was born at Edward W. Sparrow Hospital in 1932 my mother stayed there for ten days. I have a copy of the hospital bill: $78.

By the time I was ready to walk they found that I had flat feet. We don't hear a lot about that these days. I was fitted with huge, heavy orthopedic shoes, in response to which I plopped down and refused to do anything that involved moving them. One day I was outside barefoot and the miracle happened. In my baby book, Mother wrote, "She walked a whole city block the very first time she tried." I still have flat feet.

When I was older we loved to look at our feet through fluoroscopes, featured in many shoe stores. They guaranteed a perfect fit because you could see if the bones were constricted. It turned out that fluoroscopes were x-ray machines and in retrospect it was postulated that we had done untold damage to our bodies. We seem to have overcome that hazard and as far as I know none of our feet glow in the dark.

Tonsils and adenoids were lopped out as a matter of routine. When we were about 5 my brother Charles and I each had the procedure performed at a surgeon's office. An ether-drip mask was held over our faces and we were instructed to count. My brother, then in kindergarten, began, "One, two . . ." up to nine.

"Go on," said the doctor.

"That's as far as I can count," little Charles said.

After surgery we went home and stared at our promised ice cream, as painful to swallow as the spruce needles in the back yard.

Once the tonsils and adenoids were dispatched we were left to deal with other illnesses, such as mumps, whooping cough, measles, chicken pox, and scarlet fever, most of which kids are vaccinated against these days. Each brought its special miseries. For some, the department of health posted large red signs on our front doors. "Contagious Disease. Do Not Enter!" or words to that effect. Quite the status symbol. Quarantined! No school for us, often for a week or more. I remember that when we had whooping cough we went outside to admire the sign, coughing to the point of nausea.

When we had measles we weren't to be in bright light, for fear of damaging our eyes. Our father sat in the hall between our darkened bedrooms reading aloud to help pass the time. A favorite was the phrase, "Anything for a quiet life, said the little, small red hen," which he read in his resonant, most un-hen-like voice.

Illness involving nausea caused Charles to use Mother's cure. This was tomato juice mixed with salt and sugar, a noxious mess that I thought made everything worse.

Scarlet fever was a much-feared disease. My husband's older brother Bill spent weeks at the "Pest House," Lansing City Hospital, on Michigan Avenue (later annexed to Sparrow). Bill says that he was there three or four weeks, he thinks largely because his mother was pregnant at the time. He was only 7, but he recalls nearly every minute of his stay in a ward with 15 to 20 other males of all ages.

One Sunday, his father brought the comics, wrapped with a rubber band. Non-staff people weren't allowed in the wards, so he gave the paper to a nurse. She delivered it to Bill, who was delighted to find an entire pack of Teaberry gum smuggled in with the funnies.

Later, the nurse saw the gum and said, "You can't have that. We all share everything here. But," she added, "you've already touched it, so it's too late now."

Bill remembers his family standing outside the building under his window. They would smile and wave, generally making him feel loved but sadly isolated. He also says he can't drink malts, even this many years later, because his horribly bitter medicine was served mixed with malted milk.

The dark specter of polio, infantile paralysis, haunted everyone. It paralyzed children, some of whom had to live forever dependent on an iron lung. Many were severely crippled and had to use crutches for the rest of their lives. This disease spread through contact and the only effective method of control was to minimize that contact. Public swimming pools were shunned, along with crowded beaches. During summer, the peak polio season, our parents forbid movies and other activities that placed us in crowds.

We were afraid, but in the way children are – someone else might get it, not us. When I was about 12 a neighbor boy, Bobby Euwema, developed an infection that sent angry red streaks up his arm and through his shoulder. Blood poisoning! This was during World War II and a new miracle drug, sulfa (sulfanilamide) was widely used by medics on the front. Bobby was given sulfa tablets and the red streaks disappeared.

My mother said, "Only a year or two earlier, Bobby would have died. Sulfa wasn't available and there was no way to treat blood poisoning."

Her statement made a big impression on me and that memory is still vivid.

Today medical treatment makes these stories about the past seem rather quaint. Outpatient surgery is the norm for many procedures. New drugs have altered patterns of illness. Research gives us hints of what is to come, mostly good things but also some warnings about the likelihood of pandemics in our future.

We hear lots of criticism of the medical system in this country. Surely things need improvement. But many illnesses that crippled and killed are now almost forgotten.

I know my father would agree that today's population is healthier and longer-lived. Comparing medicine then and now offers the reward he promised, the advantage of seeing how things turn out.

To a Dying Man

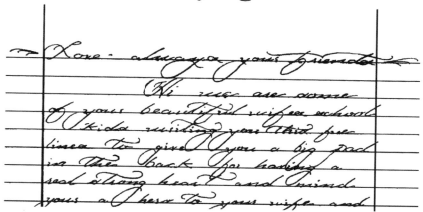

In October of 1994, it was evident that my husband, Russ, was not going to be with us much longer. He had battled cancer since January of that year, had many tests and surgery on a cancer-broken femur. He never had chemotherapy. By the time he was diagnosed, the cancer had gone from liver to bones, beating him down relentlessly.

During his illness I had been absent quite often from my teaching job at Challenger Youth Center, where Los Angeles teenagers were confined by court order for a year, on average. Finally I told my students that my husband was very ill, and that it was a matter of days – a week at most. I told of Russ's ten-month battle, how he had fought until he could fight no more.

A student named Hernandez asked, "Can we write to him?"

"I think he'd like that," I said.

Soon they handed me two letters, each written in elegant Hispanic-style script. One of them said:

"Hi. We are some of your beautiful wife's school kids writing you these few lines to give you a big pat on the back for having a real strong heart and mind. You're a hero to your wife and a legend to us because your wife talks and tells us a lot about you and the kind of man you are. You are the kind of man we need in this world now and then. As you see, I'm not a man yet, I'm still getting in trouble, but I'm trying to be a man and wishing I had the same heart you have to support your wife. And she's real happy to be with you; no matter what, you're her hero and you are our legend. God bless you."

Everyone in the class signed it, and my son, Andy, read it at Russ's funeral five days later.

In the Eye of the Beholder

*E*rma Bombeck once wrote that in her lifetime she had lost about 1200 pounds. Of course, she explained, she had probably gained 1300 pounds. In two neat sentences, she summed up my life, and perhaps the lives of many women scrabbling about in a culture that says, "Thn is beautiful "

Erma also wrote about her sagging body ("gravity wins every time"), the horrors of florescent-lighted changing rooms where new outfits never defeat greenish skin, and about battling the forces of nature that worked relentlessly on her aging body. We could relate.

Not that others aren't trying to help. There's the Scarsdale Diet, the Atkins Diet, the Zone and countless others. We have the dietary plans – Weight Watchers, Nutrisystem and the like. It's all out there. Slimness on a stick. Literally. The stick would be us, of course.

And it's not just about fat. We can also achieve better skin, glossy hair, whiter teeth. Heck, we can enjoy the wonders of Botox, liposuction and face lifts, should we choose to enter the nuclear war on aging, and if we have the means to employ those weapons of mass construction.

We women tend to lug around an image of what we're supposed to look like. Doesn't matter that we never looked like that, never will.

Does that make us ugly?

Grab a photo album and look at yourself twenty, ten, or even just a couple of years ago. Back when you first looked at those pictures, you might have been disappointed, even disgusted by your appearance.

But looking at those pictures today, at least in my case, I find that I wasn't ugly at all. What was my vision of myself then? Wrapped up in the latest *McCall's* or *Vogue* magazines, that's where. Accepting their images as an attainable, desirable goal for me was a mistake. I bought someone else's idea of beauty, even while knowing that it wasn't for me.

Today we get it from all sides. The media (to use an overworked term) continually harangues us about our appearance. It doesn't seem to care a fig about who we are as people. That attitude wouldn't sell moisturizer, white strips and hair conditioner.

With rare exceptions, only our doctors seem to worry about what's inside us, let alone whether we accept ourselves as we really are. When was the last time you heard anyone say, "I just love so-and-so. She is so flawlessly beautiful, so slim!"

When a woman friend dies, do you mourn her any less because she didn't have perfect skin? Do you ever think, "I wish she had lived her life as a really good-looking person?" Of course not.

We *are* beautiful, we need to know that. Every time we smile, we are beautiful. Every time we act with kindness, we are beautiful. Have you ever seen an ugly smile? I don't believe I ever have, not a sincere one.

Beauty lies in eyes that really see others, in ears that genuinely hear them. It is the spark that shines from those eyes, the caring that comes from a heart that is willing to give. True beauty lies in fixing our brains and our perceptions, not in worrying about how perfectly formed we are.

Someone once asked Robert Frost if he had hope for the future. He said yes, both for the future, and for the past.

Hope for the past? Indeed. Once we know enough about ourselves – why we do what we do, and why we did what we did, we can forget what we never quite achieved and concentrate on being ourselves.

A friend, one of the most self-confident and selfless people I know, recently told me, "I discovered that I could accept myself years ago when I found out I wasn't going to die." She had suffered a mastectomy and massive amounts of chemotherapy before she finally received assurance that she would be allowed to live to raise her small sons. "All my life until then, I had tried to fit in, to be liked, to be the person I thought that I should be, because that's the way others expected me to be. But as I left the hospital I thought, 'I can't waste energy on that stuff any longer. I'm just going to try to be the best person that I know how to be.'" She added, "I knew then and there that I could do it, that I was free as I had never been before."

In fixing our messages to ourselves, we can begin to accept parts of us that are splotchy, flabby, skinny, achy, even missing. We can better deal with our reality because we will know who we are. Our hearts and minds will tell us. And when they do, they will love us.

Unconditionally.

Rebel Unaware

*I*n 1936 at age four I entered kinder-garten at East Lansing's Bailey School. They weren't too fussy about age then, and my mother decided that because I was so big I should start school. "You used to mother them all [the other kids] ," she would say fondly.

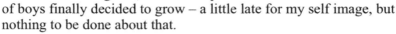

I wasn't five until the end of April that year. I was the biggest kid in my class until fourth grade, when a couple of boys finally decided to grow – a little late for my self image, but nothing to be done about that.

One late fall day that year our kindergarten teacher, Miss Dialy, said we were going to make paper squirrels. She distributed brown paper and scissors and said, "Now, Boys and Girls, cut out a squirrel."

Freehand? In kindergarten? Kindergartners can't stay inside the lines with crayon. What made her think we could cut out a squirrel freehand? Some of the kids began to cry as their scissors amputated intended limbs and tails, slicing and snipping in all the wrong places.

I didn't know about hand-eye coordination at that age, but I did know that everyone was upset. And I also knew I couldn't cut out a squirrel. I lopped about an inch off the top of the paper, leaving a tab in the center of the top.

"Here's my squirrel," I told my teacher. "That's its head," pointing to the tab.

"Clarice," she said severely, "You need to try. If you can't make an effort you'll have to stay in at recess time." Fine with me; I was done with squirrels.

Attached to the classroom was a narrow, dark, hook-lined coatroom. Most coats were tossed onto hooks. Mittens and wet footwear littered the floor. There was a strong smell of wet wool. This windowless coatroom was where you stayed if you were kept in from recess.

At least it wasn't solitary confinement. A skinny-legged, knock-kneed little kid, Tommy Bondy, had also apparently sinned during the morning. He and I were to remain in the coatroom until the class returned from recess.

I knew that on that particular day my mother had some sort of appointment and I was to go to the neighbor's house across the street when we got out of school at around noon. I liked to go there. Mr. Cahill was a widower, and his housekeeper was a kind woman. I had never gone there alone. This was a rare treat and I decided it was quite unnecessary to put it off. I had both motive and opportunity. Perfect.

"Let's go home," I said to Tommy. Tommy was pretty uncertain about that idea, but somehow I convinced him it was the logical thing to do. So we donned our coats and boots, said goodby as we parted outside the school and went our separate ways.

My mother collected me at Cahill's, gave me lunch and settled me for my regular nap – "Rest," she called it. Kindergarten kids didn't take naps – and I strongly suspect the rest was for my mother as much as for me.

Later, when she opened my bedroom door, a glance at her face told me I was in big trouble. The school had called, apparently having figured out I was AWOL. I suppose there were consequences for me, but I don't remember for sure. I think, in retrospect, there were consequences for Miss Dialy. I must have made my point about freehand paper art somewhere along the line. At any rate, the teacher handled me with extreme care thereafter. On my mother's birthday she set me to making a necklace for my mother of elbow macaroni and squares of colored paper. No one else ever got to do that, as far as I can recall.

Tommy Bondy changed schools shortly after that. Maybe they sent him to reform school. I got along pretty well, save for a few minor scrapes, until third grade when I dumped the dead classroom goldfish in the girls' bathroom sink. The teacher never said anything about toilets, she just told me to dump the goldfish.

Being a kid isn't easy.

You Can Do It – Maybe

*W*e all have our idols. One of mine is the handyman. I have admired his workbench, outfitted with everything he needs. Above the bench a pegboard boasts silhouettes of each tool to show exactly where it should hang. The workbench is as pristine as a tropical beach.

The dream handyman wears creased jeans. He owns roughly $100 thousand worth of tools – routers, various saws, things called jigs – wonderful devices that make it all seem so very easy. He does not get dirty, pound his thumb or make mistakes.

Naturally he and his workshop are seen on TV or in magazines. Reality is quite another thing.

Here's a rule for starting any home improvement project – be sure your gas tank is full. Even the smallest projects invariably seem to require a trip to the hardware store. If you want a truth to hang onto, there it is – any home repair project means a trip, or multiple trips, to the store.

Maybe you want to add a coat of paint to a bathroom wall, tighten a wobbling closet door or try something as ambitious as installing the gate that you never got around to when you built the fence – five years ago. Whatever it is, it will eventually necessitate a trip to the workbench.

Yes, the workbench. That would be the table-like object in the garage or basement, the one piled high with power tools, gritty flower pots, and dozens of tiny brown bags from past projects, unlabeled and for the most part unidentifiable. If your project requires, say, a 1-1/4" #12 screw and your workbench is as described, you won't be able to find one. You will find lots of ripped shrink-wrapped packages with one or two unused items trapped like ancient flies in amber. On opening the brown bags you might find dust, lint, perhaps a nail, washer, door stop or molly bolt. But not in a million tries will you find that 1-1/4" #12 screw. Off to the hardware store you go.

My daughter claims that hardware guys use those little brown sacks for small objects because we'll give up the hunt after opening a few that have been sitting around for years.

Hardware people understand that we will eventually figure out that it will take longer to search through all those little sacks than it will to make a run to their stores.

They also know that once in the store, you are susceptible to the Hardware Siren. She's invisible, of course, her voice inaudible, but she does the job. Before you know it you are admiring garbage disposal cleaning pellets, musical door chimes and – get this – a battery powered tape measure that shoots the tape to the opposite side of whatever large object you wish to measure.

You look at vinyl hoses, cookware, screen repair kits, doormats, plungers and many other things designed to mesmerize the hapless I-just-want-one-thing customer.

Back home with several suddenly-necessary items, including that tape measure, you search the shopping bag (plastic, not paper) for the screws. Oh, no. Forgot the screws. No one has heard you come in, so it is still possible to put everything back into the car and return to the store. No harm, no foul. You successfully silence the inner voice that says, "Coward. Senile forgetful person. How childish to go slinking back to the store without telling anyone."

On your return, armed with the newly purchased screw (you had to buy a package of eight, but best not to quibble) you look for the tool. In a drawer neatly labeled "screw drivers" you actually find one. What a boost to the sagging ego!

You notice that it happens to be a Phillips head screwdriver. You look at the screw. Slotted as they come. Not to worry, there are screwdrivers of all persuasions everywhere in the house. The search begins. "Honey, have you seen . . .?"

Honey never has, and if Honey is smart he or she will have nothing to do with this. "Nope. No. Never. Not me. You had one the day you forgot your key and broke the lock on the back door. Red handle? I never saw a red-handled screwdriver in this house."

No need to outline the agonies of the search. Just know that soon you are on your way again to buy screwdriver number 52. And this one will go into that drawer where it won't get lost.

And it won't rain in April.

In workshop Nirvana all drills are charged, all nails and screws sorted and secured, all sawdust trapped in neat little bags. We know how it is done.

But, even so, it is probably a good idea to be sure that the gas tank is full.

Good Eye

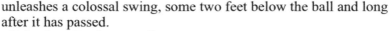

*I*t's Freddy's turn at bat in his little league game. He pushes his thick glasses up on his nose and takes his batting stance, hips wiggling, bat planted far too firmly on his shoulder.

The first pitch is about three feet to the left of the plate. He does not swing.

"Good eye, Fred Baby," we shout from the stands.

The next pitch is in almost exactly the same place, but Freddy unleashes a colossal swing, some two feet below the ball and long after it has passed.

"It"s okay, Fred," we yell.

"More to come."

Freddy fails to swing sufficient times to be awarded a walk. After the game, we congratulate him on his stellar performance. We recognize that he's learning and we want him to feel confident, to enjoy the process. Never mind the 25 - 6 score.

Melissa teeters perilously at the Kiddie Ballet performance of "Cinderella." We don't care, she looks like an angel and we thoroughly enjoy that *she* thoroughly enjoys what she is doing.

At his piano recital, Bobby holds the sustain pedal down through his entire performance of "Dancing Clowns." The clowns definitely do not dance. Even so, as Bobby rushes by on his way to the punch bowl we congratulate him on his fine musicianship.

But something happens along the way to adulthood. Fred doesn't make the varsity baseball team and feels himself a failure. At the high school musical, Melissa is asked to help with the props; the teacher explains that it's not that she isn't a good dancer; they really do need help finding chairs and lamps. And Bob's Aunt Susie tells him that she thought he played somewhat "heavily," with the school orchestra.

As adults we seem to have decided that perfection is not only desirable, but achievable. If it isn't perfect, it isn't really very good.

There's another side of the picture that needs to be examined, however. It's the joy factor, the love of the process that we need to keep in mind. Sometimes flaws are more interesting than perfection.

At a high school musical production, the audience is rapt. Not only because it is good, but because every single time someone successfully reaches that high note, it's a home run. The high school performance is far more full of soul than a professional production, or a movie that achieves perfection through re-takes and skilled editing.

The community band gives a concert in the park. We wince at the occasional squeak, the cymbal crash in a triple-piano passage. We tend to hear the squeaks and the crash and fail to see the joy, the pride of the players who are happily doing what they love. If they were fourth-graders, we would be thrilled that they were happily doing what they loved. But it is easy to think that these are adults; they shouldn't be making mistakes. Mistakes ruin the performance. It's not the process that counts, it's the result.

A friend delivered her PhD thesis for printing. "I know it will have some typos," she fretted. What she couldn't see was that after retirement she embarked on a PhD program, spent six years taking courses, doing research and producing an excellent 300-page thesis. All that, and she worried about typos.

Fact is, life is filled with typos in one form or another. Nothing is perfect. No human endeavor is without flaws. We need to remind ourselves that life is a process.

How boring it would be if the finished product were perfect. There would be nothing left to work on, no flaws to work out, nothing to do but admire our work and then look around for something that needs fixing.

If we were lucky enough to find that thing, I hope that during the process someone would come along, admire our work and say, "Good eye!"

Celebrating Family

Come summer, Americans like to reune. Yes, reune. It's a real word which means having a reunion. I found it in my crossword dictionary.

Families reune, as do alumni, military and many other groups. Often these gatherings are outdoor affairs. The reason seems obvious. Children cavorting near Staffordshire china and other treasures can create havoc. Serious reunion hosts rent Andy Gumps. If you don't know what those are, you've never been to a California outdoor festival.

Recently my husband Jack's extended family met at a farm near Alma for its annual reunion. The family name, Church, has prevailed in America for many, many years. Willard Church was a drummer in the Army of the Revolution. He named his son Lafayette, in honor of the French general of the American Revolution.

Lafayette married Sophronia Benjamin in 1840 and, during the Civil War, was a chaplain with the American army. The Church family reunions began within a couple of decades after the war, at Lafayette and Sofronia's farm near Alma, Michigan.

If there is a more delicious name than Sophronia I have yet to hear it. The family also boasted an Avolin (male), and an Ersaldine (female), who detested the name and fought, mostly unsuccessfully, to be called "Sally." She used to perform handstands but has given them up, since she is 89 years old.

When I first met Ersaldine eight years ago she offered to demonstrate the art for us. Someone said, "That's okay, Ersaldine, we wouldn't want to be responsible if something went wrong."

"Well, I could do it, you know," she grumbled. No one doubted that for a moment.

Reunions bring out the chef in nearly everyone. The Churches simply couldn't do without Ersaldine's pecan tarts (made by daughter Janet in recent years) and Kathleen's wonderful meatballs simmering in their crock pot.

Salads run from pea-peanut to pasta to Jello. Rich chocolate cakes, whipped cream concoctions and summer fruits make a dramatic show on the table. There's plenty for everyone – thirds and fourths, in fact.

Posted on a barn wall is the family tree, starting with Layfatte and Sophronia and running to the babies of the current generation – an impressive 9 or 10 feet long. Pens and sticky pads are available for anyone with information to add, or correct.

This year several newcomers arrived, receiving joyous receptions. None were named Church, but they were somebody's great-something, or cousin thrice removed. Didn't matter, they brought new perspectives and details to add to the family tree. And of course, they brought wonderful food.

Sated after dinner, we sat beneath the trees and discussed our current lives along with anecdotes about those who are no longer with us.

There was talk of Francis Pharcellus Church (Cousin Frank), who wrote the editorial "Yes Virginia, There Is a Santa Claus," for the *New York Sun* in 1897. He spent many summers on the farm. Jack and I named our cat "Pharcella" to honor him, since we acquired her on the 100th anniversary of the editorial.

Other names that came up in conversation were Barbara (Jack's mother) and her cousins – Max-and-Carl (always said as one word), Neal, Mary, Nellie, Harly, Ruth, Kate, Howard, Addie, Arthur, Bert, Bruce, Frances, Florence, Volney. They had been parents, grandparents or great-grandparents of many of the group.

Later, some families prepared to leave and, began to summon their children.

"No, not yet!" cried Janet. "We haven't taken the group picture."

The herding process began and, after long minutes, we were assembled, more or less facing the camera. The ritual posing was punctuated by people dashing from the group to hand cameras to the designated photographer.

"Okay, now. Everyone. Smile!" he cried, again and again. Thus our group photo joined a long line of similar ones stretching back more than a century.

Now, Jack and I are of the oldest generation. Although we are dressed differently than those in long-ago photos, our facial expressions are much the same. Our feelings are probably similar, since we share a sense of continuity and well-being.

Lafayette and Sophronia lie in a tiny cemetery where two dirt roads meet, less than a mile from the farm. How amazed they would be to see our lives today. How proud they would be to know that they remain a vital part of this day's celebration

Cooking with Joy

I take my *Joy of Cooking* book off its shelf with two hands. It must be cradled, since the back, spine and front cover have almost completely separated from the text.

In the 1960s, when my book first developed serious health problems, our kitchen sported orange, gold and avocado green flowered wall-paper, with matching curtains. The late 1950s and early '60s were a heyday for those colors. Stoves, refrigerators and enamel sinks were avocado, an artsy term for pea soup green. I covered the book with fabric left over from my curtain sewing. It still wears this cover, though the fabric is stained and scuffed, disgusting enough to discourage the heartiest appetite.

I once read of a woman who came to care for a family when the wife and mother was ill. She knew exactly what to cook for them. She searched out the most tattered and stained recipe cards and cookbook pages. It worked perfectly. If she came to my house, she would be hard pressed because in 50 years' time, nearly every page of my *Joy* has become stained, and all of them are tattered.

In 1954 no one had heard the term "lite." We couldn't possibly set the food processor on "pulse" since the only pulse we knew was in charge of our circulation. Recipes in the book speak of whole cream, butter, and sugar. Sugar substitute would have been honey, corn syrup or perhaps brown sugar. "Equal" meant "on a par with." Dedicated cooks made Sunshine Cake with seven egg yolks, using the seven whites to whip up an Angel Food cake. Seven egg yolks sounded about right, then. If anyone knew about cholesterol, word hadn't reached America's homemakers.

At the back of the book there's a section called Cooking and Kitchen Hints. It is a list of kitchen necessities, including a malted milk shaker, an ice cream freezer, a set of refrigerator containers, and – for time-saving – an electric mixer, a blender and a pressure cooker. No mention of food processor, coffee grinder, bagel slicer, espresso machine or ice crusher. Microwave ovens wouldn't appear until the late 1960s.

The Meat section discusses the modern way of roasting, using consistently low temperatures. There are instructions on soaking a ham and drawing poultry. In 1954 everyone knew that drawing poultry meant getting the intestines out. The intestines weren't in tidy little giblet bags – they were intestines. However, in 1954, pre-cleaned and packaged poultry could be purchased, at least in larger towns and cities. A friend remembers that around that time his mother proudly said that she'd just bought a six-legged chicken!

Over the years a few extraneous papers have infiltrated the pages of the book. From the 1970s there's a crayon drawing done by one of my children in lots of purple, red and orange. "Peace," it says. "It comes in all shapes and sizes." The artist strengthened the motif by drawing peace signs in all shapes and sizes.

From the same era, I have kept a note written by a child who really had something to say:

FOR THE REST OF THIS DAY.
I am not TO BE DISTUREBED.
THIS DOOR [bedroom, no doubt] IS NOT TO BE TOUCHED.
ALTHOUGH THIS IS A PURE COMMUNIZED HOUSE
I DON'T WANT TO BE BRAINED INTO BEING A SLAVE.
IS THAT CLEAR!!!!!!!!!!!!

The kid had slave issues, I assume. But, no. Not possible. That was long before everyone had issues.

There's a chart from a fish store in Matlacha, Florida with directions for cooking seafood. I added some phonetic information so I wouldn't sound stupid when I shopped there, scribbling "matt-la-shay" at the top. And from my E-Z-V roaster purchase I've kept a time and temperature chart that never fails – not in some 40 years, anyway.

Recipes in today's publications tell me to turn my food processor to pulse or puree. I don't own a food processor. I am the food processor. These recipes often call for lite ingredients. When I use lite anything, the results never seem quite right. I'm hopelessly old fashioned. I have many other cookbooks – celebrity cookbooks, various ethnic books, a *Time-Life* series from the 1970s, spiral-bound fund raising efforts from various groups, the "best" recipes of everything from fairs to dorm food.

But my Joy is the most loved because it never fails to offer memories and to produce edible evidence that I haven't entirely lost my joy.

Songs of My Father As He Spoke

Segments of a taped converstion with Charles Russell Hoffer (1892-1977) on his 84th and last birthday, October 17, 1976

• On Birthdays

Well, the first one that I can remember about birthdays was that I was 12 years old and my mother and I had been out milking the cows. And we were carrying the milk up to the granary there where they had a separator.

And she said, "Do you know what day this is?"

I said, "No, I don't know what it is."

"Well," she said, "this is your birthday." And that was that.

• On Hog Butchering

Then you see you'd have to take care of the meat, dress them, hang them up. Then you have to cut them. And you cut them up into hams, bacon, and there's a certain amount of meat that goes into sausage. You'd usually make the sausage at night. Kind of a semi party, you know.

• A Day With a Cart

Once, for a while, for some reason I had a cart. You know what a cart is? A two-wheeled thing with a seat on it. And somehow you didn't have anything for your feet And I couldn't put my books anywhere. So I, one Sunday afternoon, I got busy and thought I'd nail some burlap there and make a kind of a basket on the cart. And I got that nailed and I thought, "Well, I'll get in there and see how it is." I had the shafts that go by the horse, I had them up on a wagon about the same height. And I came and got in there and sat down. And – UP! went the shafts!

• On Automobiles

I know I can remember the first car I ever saw. And the first one that went by our house. And the first one we ever got. It was a 1912 Flanders car, made by Studebaker. And then the Model T Ford came out. There's all kinds of jokes about the Ford. A kind of dirty joke in a way, but the radiators used to leak, And if you'd drive a Ford car up to stop it, maybe there'd be some water there, you know. So the joke got around, "Well, the little fellows don't know any better than that."

• On The Future

Somewhere about the time I was in sixth grade at the one-room
public school one mile west of our home, the idea emerged in my mind
that it would be advantageous to go to the Agricultural College at
Purdue University. I am unable to locate the sources of this desire.
When I got to considering occupations I was a senior in high school or
something.There were three things that played in my mind.

One was farming, I liked that.

The second was school teaching.

Third was the ministry. But the ministry didn't quite pull enough.

So that left teaching, school teaching.

• On Heating the Farmhouse

The winters were really bad and we didn't have anything like
automatic heat. The most they could get would be a hard coal burner.
And then you could get hard coal or soft coal. Hard coal burners were
covered on the outside with what you used to call isinglass, something
you could see through. It would look like there was a nice big fire
there. But what we had for heat mostly was wood. I'd go to school on
Monday, Tuesday, Thursday, Friday and on Saturday you cut wood.
I could be so dead tired Saturday night from cutting wood. You know,
enough to last for the week, for the stove, kitchen. Has to be pretty
good. Sticks that would go into the stove. Many a time when you're
going to cook a meal you'd have to start the fire. That's the only way
you're going to get it. Start it with corn cobs.

• On Farm Horses

When they got too old or you didn't want them, you'd sell them and
get something else. Or there would be some colts coming along.
When my grandparents were on a farm they had a sale – they were
going to move into Plymouth [Indiana] and they had two colts up for
sale, for auction. And my father bid 25 dollars apiece and he got them.
Nobody else put a bid in. Well we had those, they grew up. One of
them we kept, was a very, very dependable horse. He got to be almost
a member of the family. I don't know how long we had him. A long
time. And – good horse. We used to drive him to school and things
like that.

• On Storing Food
Well, you could bury potatoes. You'd put them into a pile, put straw
or hay on them and cover them with dirt. At least six inches or so. So
it wouldn't freeze through. If it got so you had to have some potatoes,
sometimes you'd dig a little hole and stuff it back up after you got
your potatoes. And I guess you could bury cabbage, too. We never
did that. The main thing you had in those days to provide something
resembling fresh vegetables would be sauerkraut. And we used to
make a barrel of sauerkraut. That's just cut up cabbage with a lot of
salt in it. I guess it just keeps. But the great thing is, you got along.

• On Courtship and Marriage
I think what was the biggest year in my life, I didn't realize it then,
was 1925. Because then I was able to finish up the [University of
Minnestoa PhD] degree, the thesis, took the examination, was
awarded the degree. And also the previous summer I'd met Luella
[Holmes]. And then soon after that, about that same time, I got the
offer to come to Michigan State. The day I got the letter I was in
Windom where Luella was a county nurse. Southern part of the state.
And we decided to, to, ah, become engaged. And so you see all that
happened in about six months. I didn't realize it then, But it sure was
going high, wide and handsome! Of course it was the culmination of a
lot of things. First I wanted someone that had farm experience. And I
wanted somebody who could make up their mind and know why they
made it up. I'd had some experience with one young lady that couldn't
do that. Never did make up her mind. And then I wanted somebody
who had an orientation towards science. Like a nurse would have. And
I didn't want somebody who was off on a flight of something or other,
you know. And then I was also interested in somebody who had an
interest in homemaking. She filled the bill! So what the heck!

Colophon

The body type in this book was set in
11 point Times New Roman TrueType,
originally created for *The Times* of London
in 1931by Victor Lardent, based on an older
type, Plantin.

Heads are 22 point Times New Roman bold,
subheads, 11 point Times New Roman italic.
The type and graphics were created with
CorelDraw 11, converted to
Portable Document Format (PDF)
using Nuance (Scansoft) Create! 6.

This page traditionally contains a brief biography of the author. The thing is, this whole book is biography. To condense it into a few short paragraphs is to be reminded of the many gifts that I have received. It's as if the Fairy of Golden Opportunities said to me, "Here you go, girl. Now try not to mess up."

– Clarice Hoffer Thompson

Starting with my parents, a college professor and registered nurse, and a brother two years older, a constant in my life, it should be easy not to mess up. There is also an excellent education in East Lansing, Michigan, schools and a bachelor's degree from Michigan State College. Add to that an MA from George Peabody College for Teachers, now part of Vanderbilt University in Nashville, Tennessee.

If that's not richness enough, my life was and is heavy with music, playing the viola in high school, then college, then various orchestras, including the Nashville Symphony, and later many local orchestras in the Los Angeles area.

These days I'm an appreciative spectator.

Teaching vocal music in several Los Angeles junior high schools offered the challenge of managing choirs of 70 or more, plus music appreciation classes, and attempting to understand these embryonic adults.

In later years, teaching in Los Angeles County Probation Department facilities brought awareness of the difficult lives these teen-age clients faced on the "outs"– outside the safer, controlled environment of prison.

Three husbands, Bob the musician, father of my children, 22 years together, then not.

Russ, jack-of-all trades, sharing for 17 years a fluid mix of various jobs and locations, spiced by playing with motorcycles until cancer took over and won.

Now, Jack, a fellow 1949 high school graduate, who drew me back to my East Lansing roots, and waters them daily. Graphic artist Jack is the miracle of this book.

Enriching our lives exponentially are my son, Andy and grandson, Rob, my daughter, Erica, her husband, Randy, and sons, Carl and Keith, as well as Jack's son Chris, wife, Wendy, and young Ethan and Sarah.

Made in the USA
Charleston, SC
11 October 2012